THIS BOOK BELONGS TO

____

Imprint: Independently published
ISBN: 9798867483661

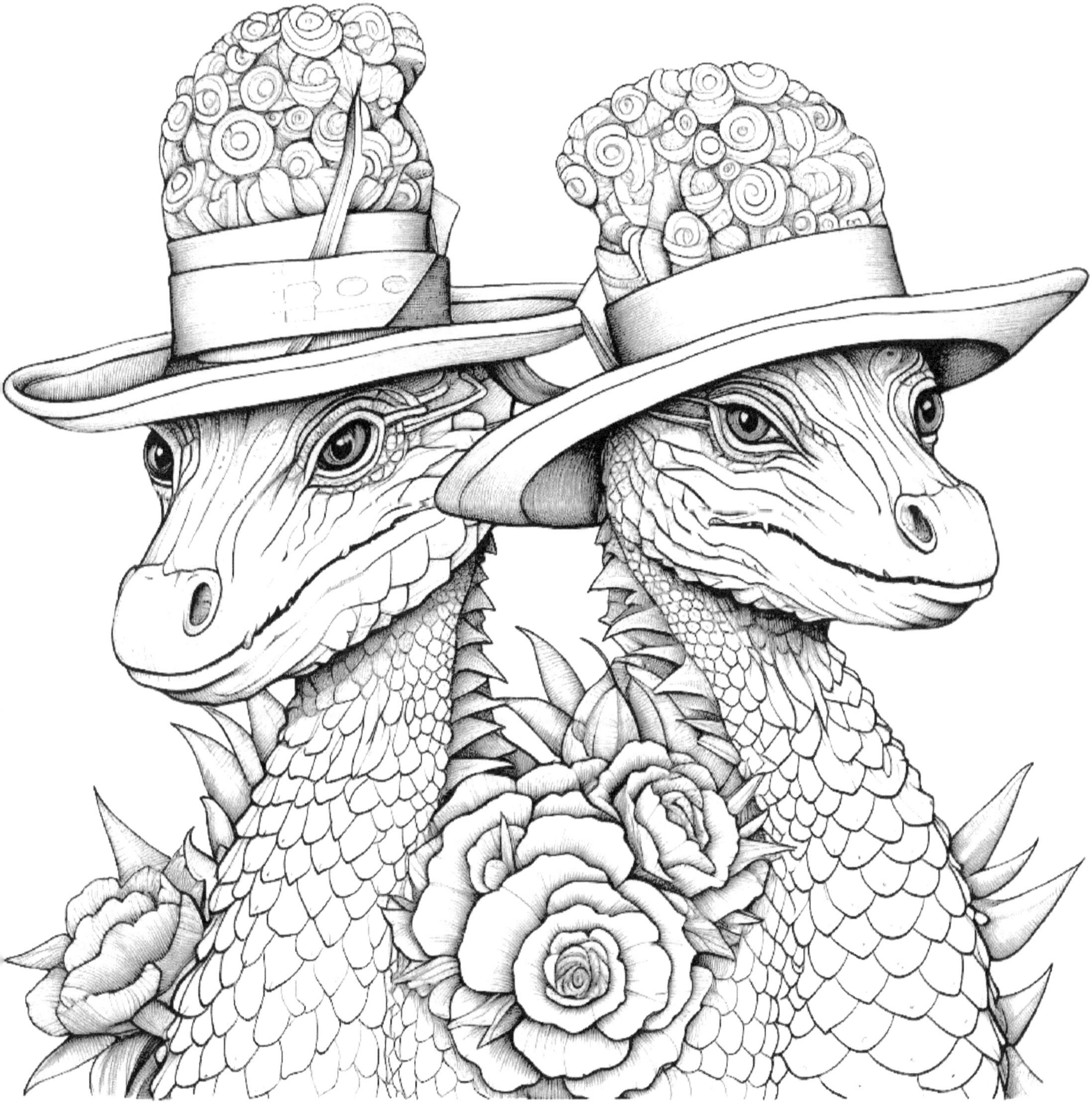

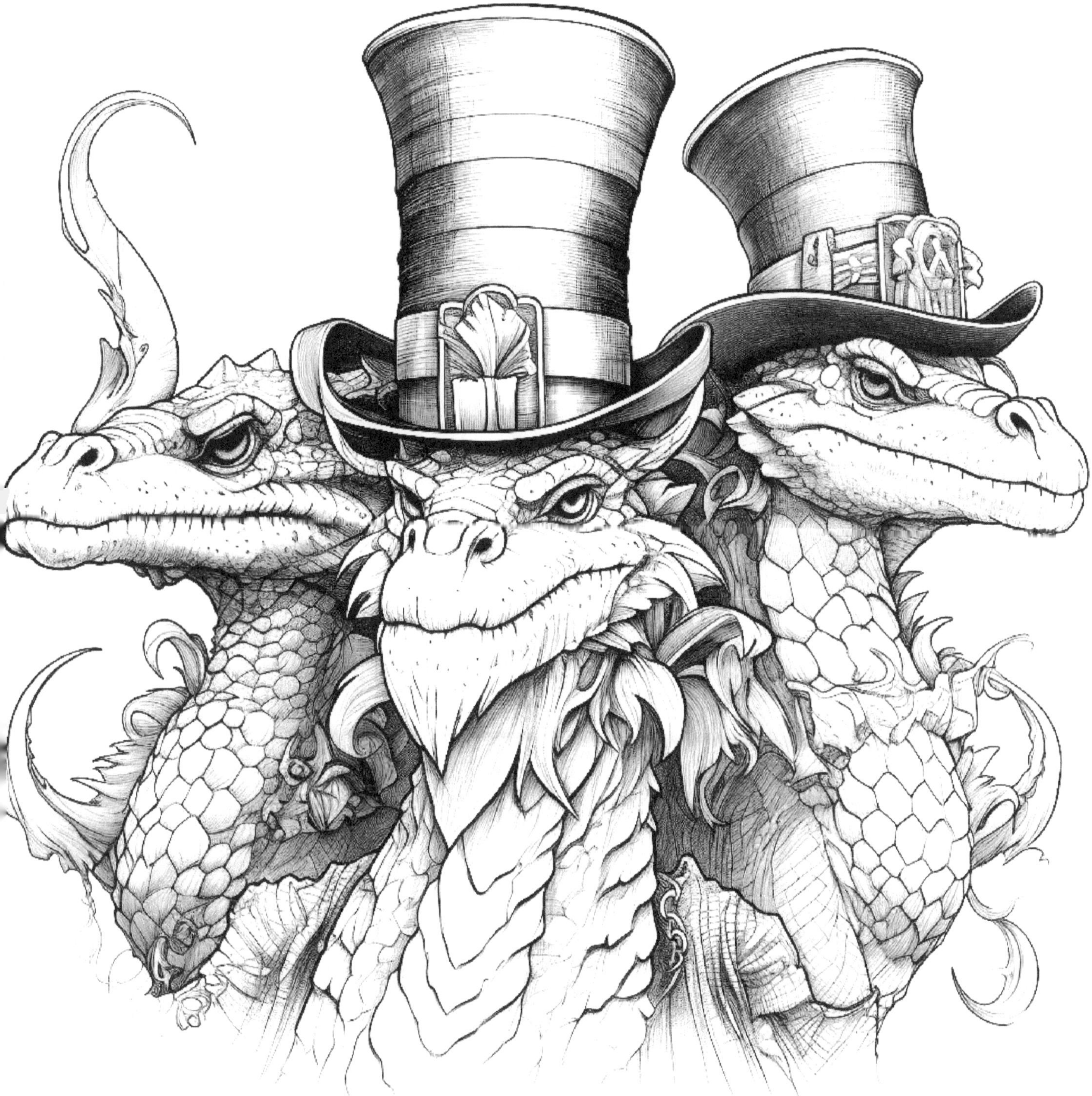

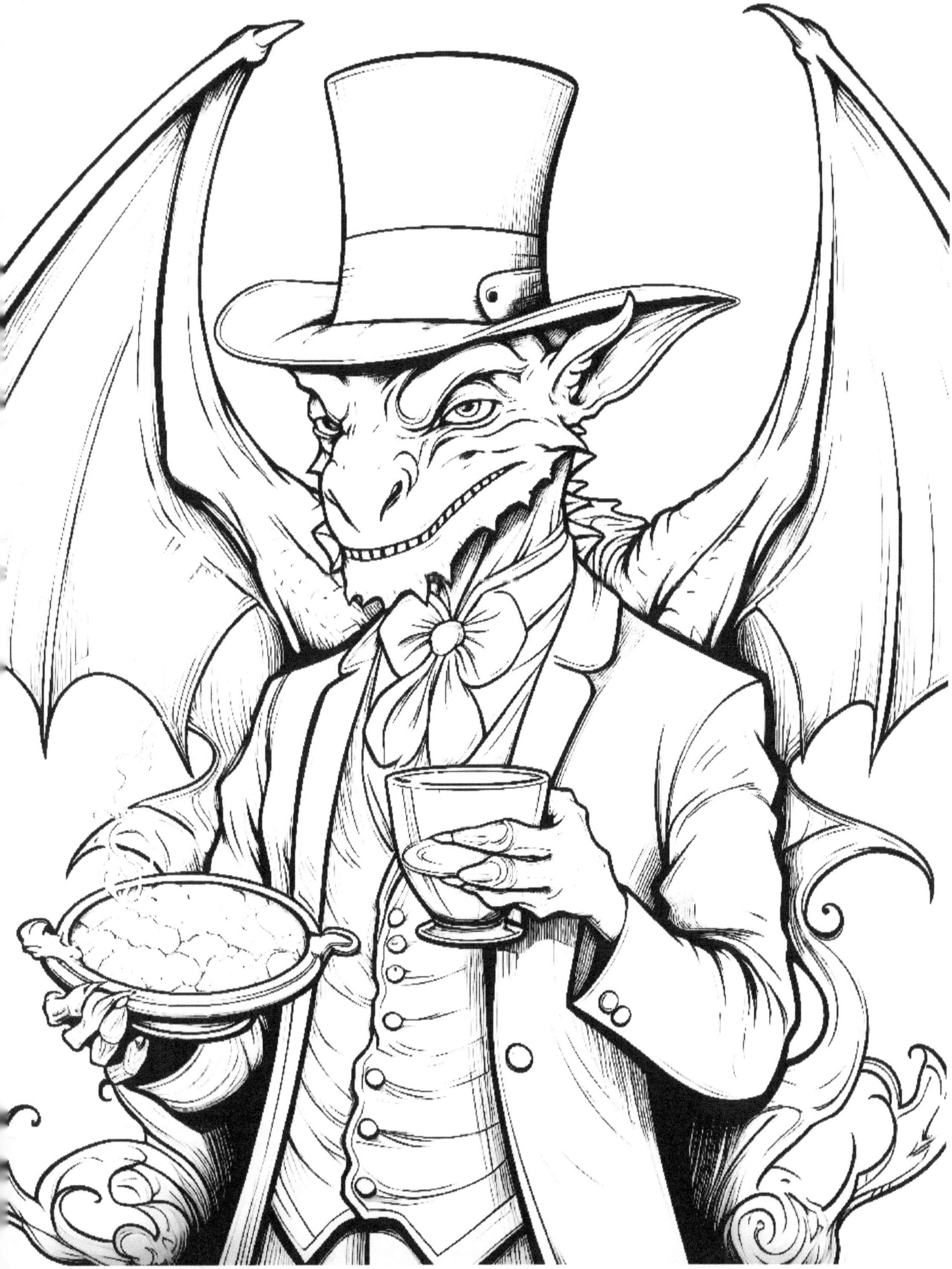

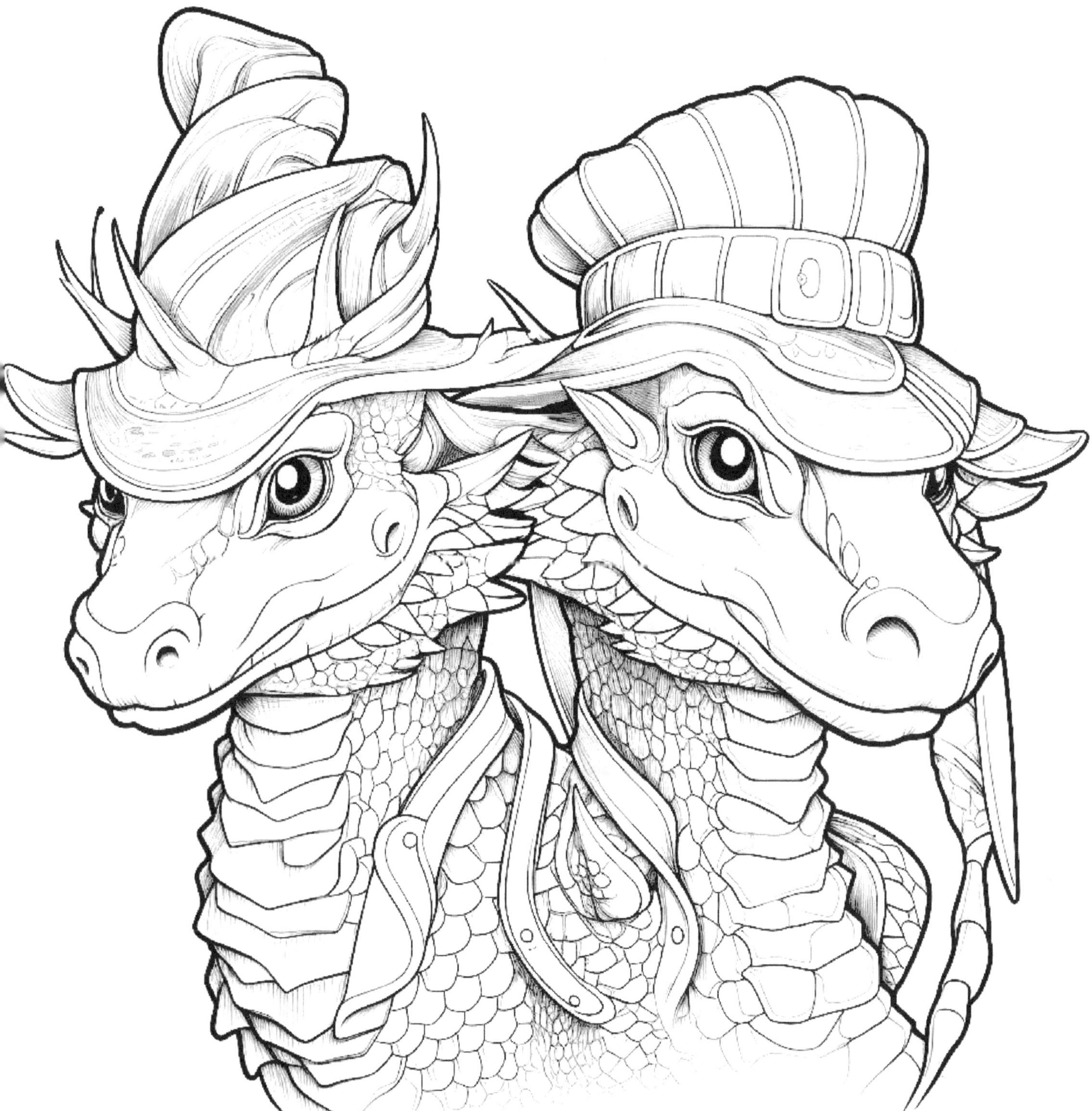

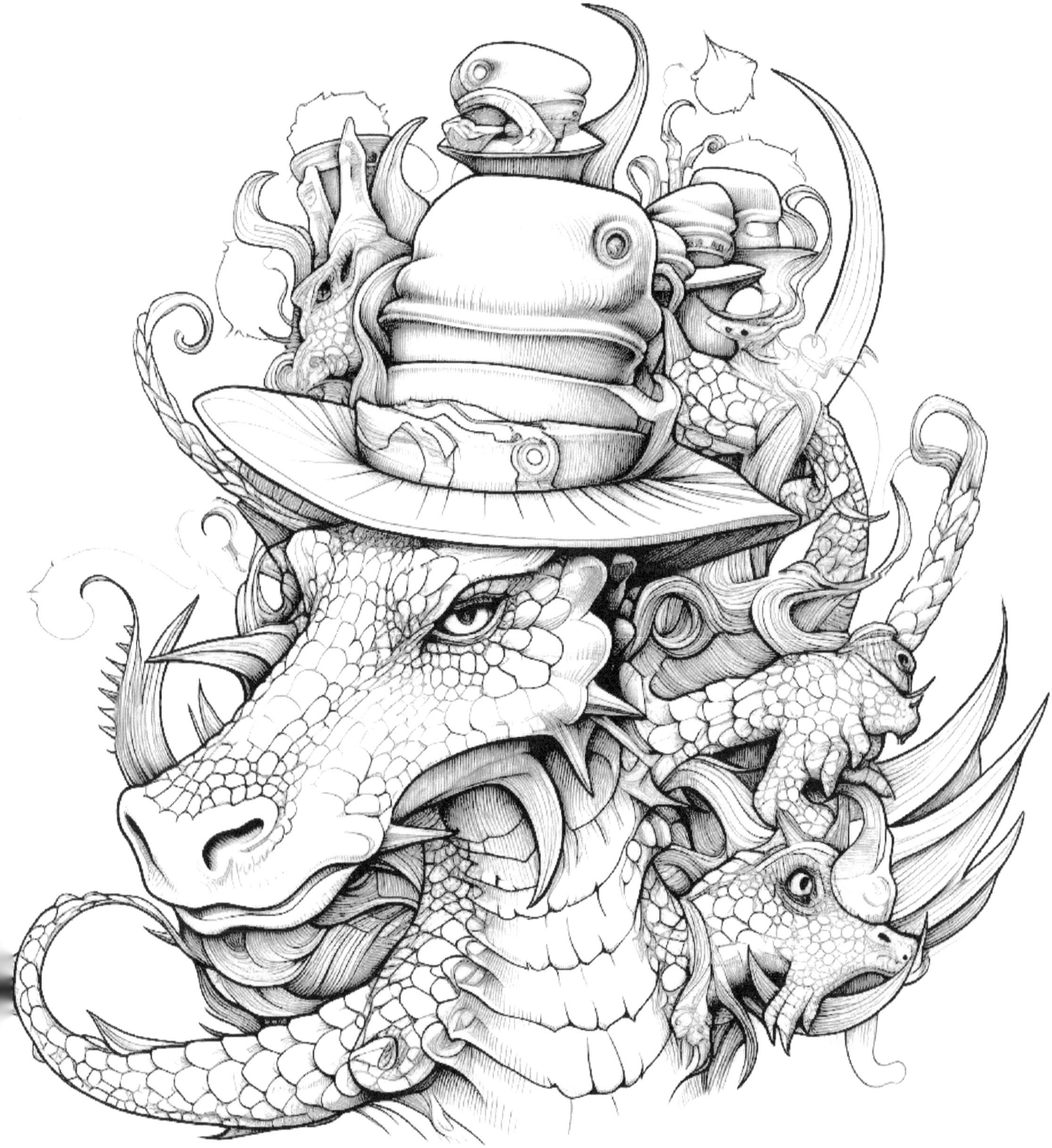

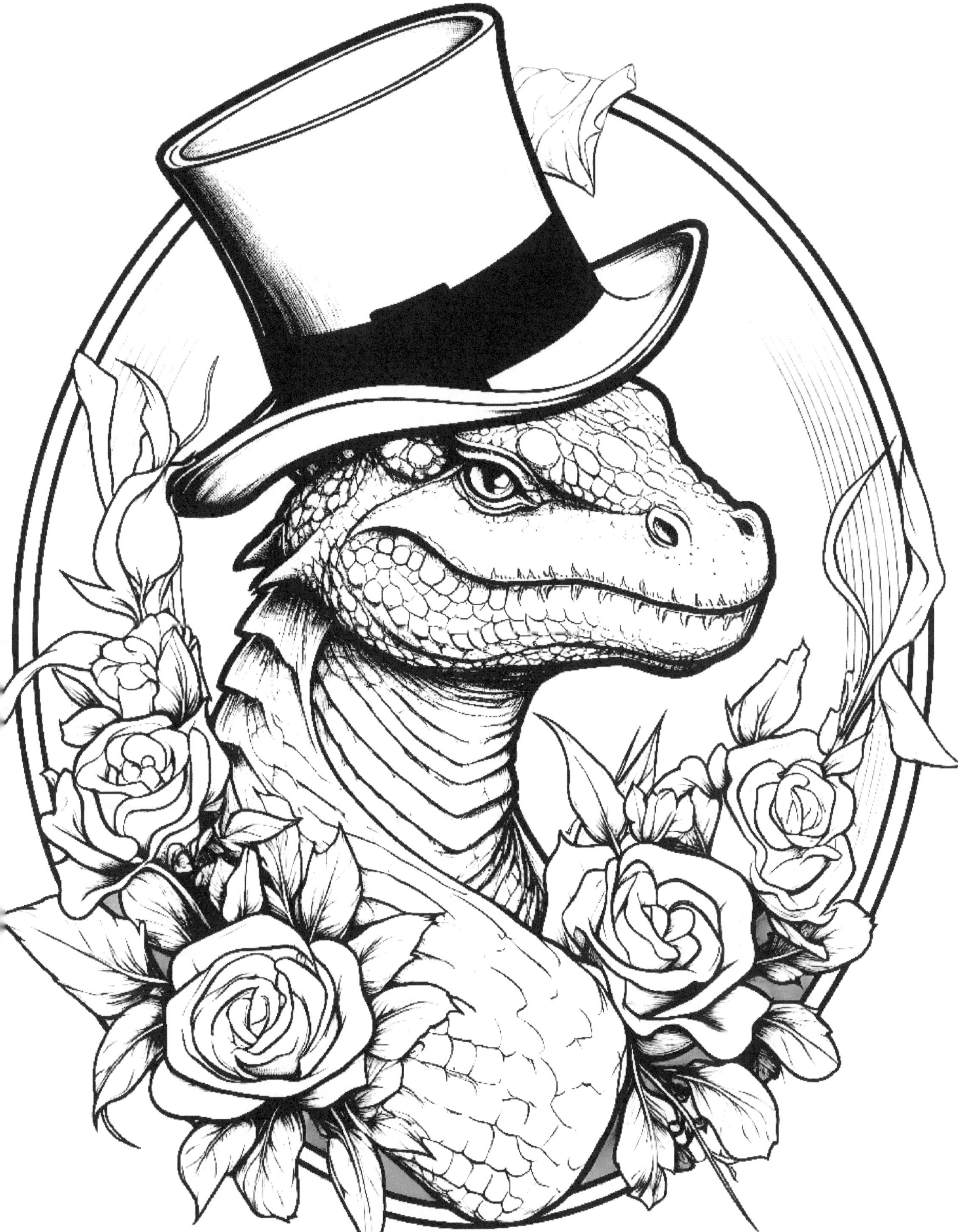

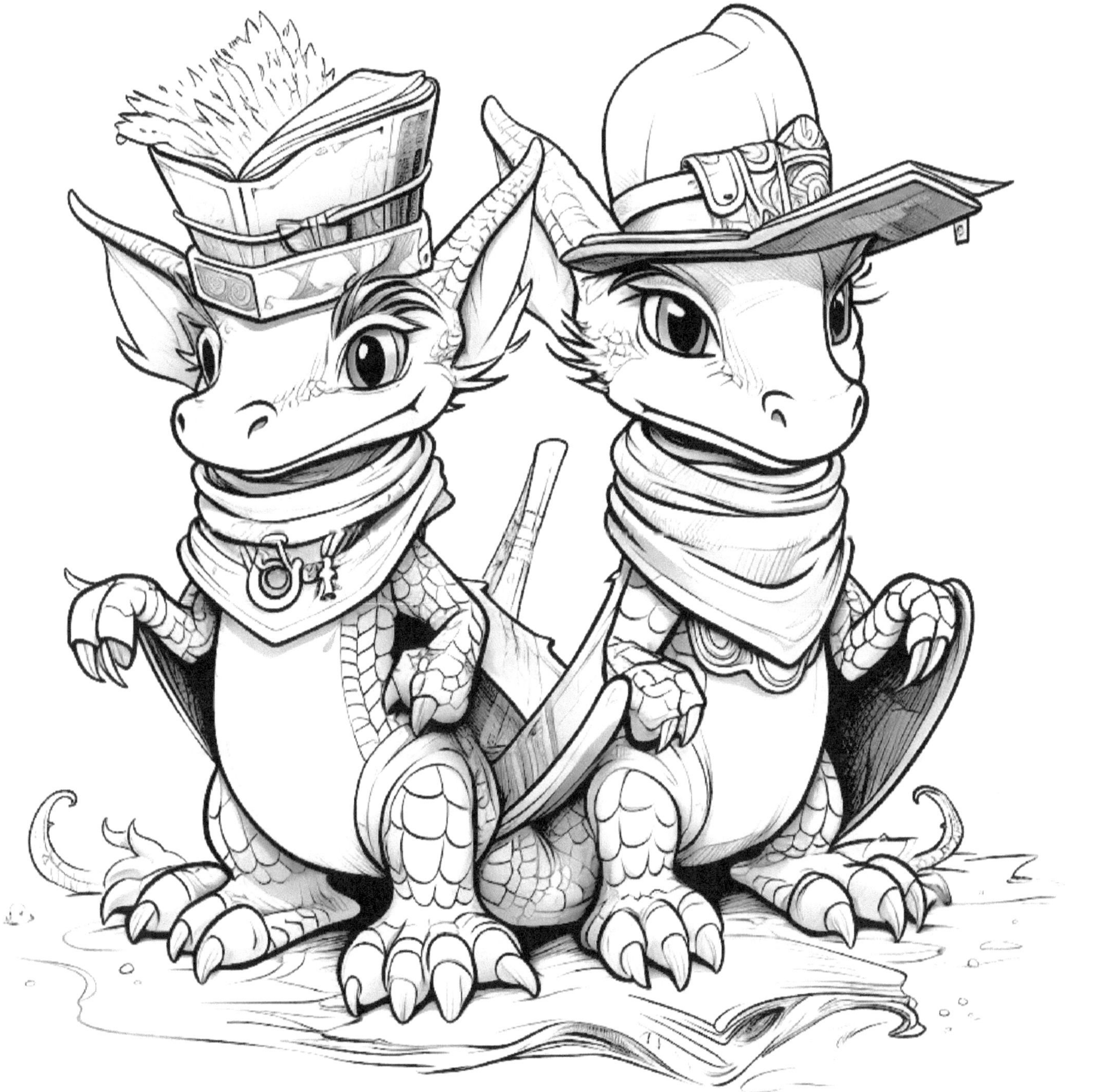

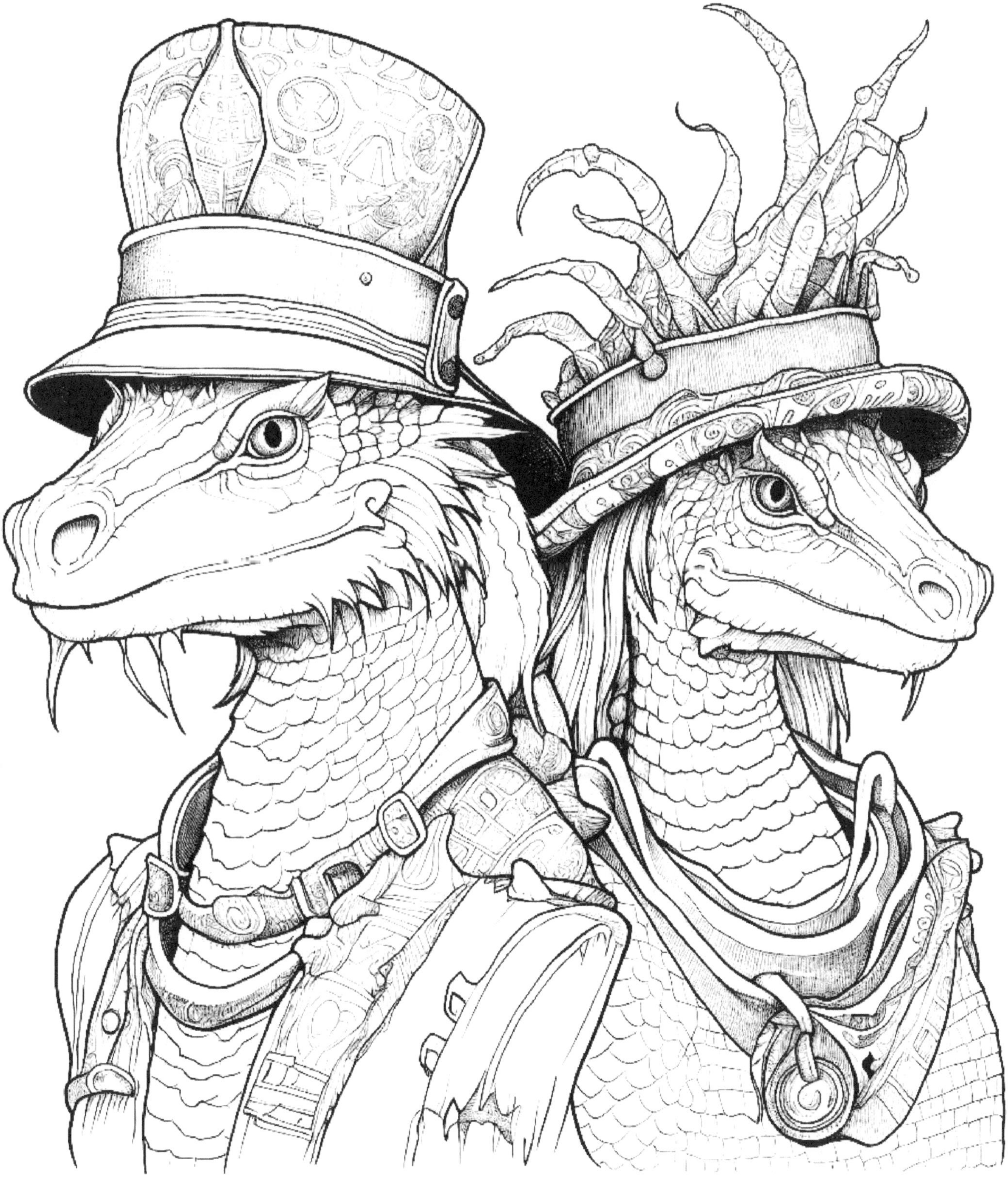

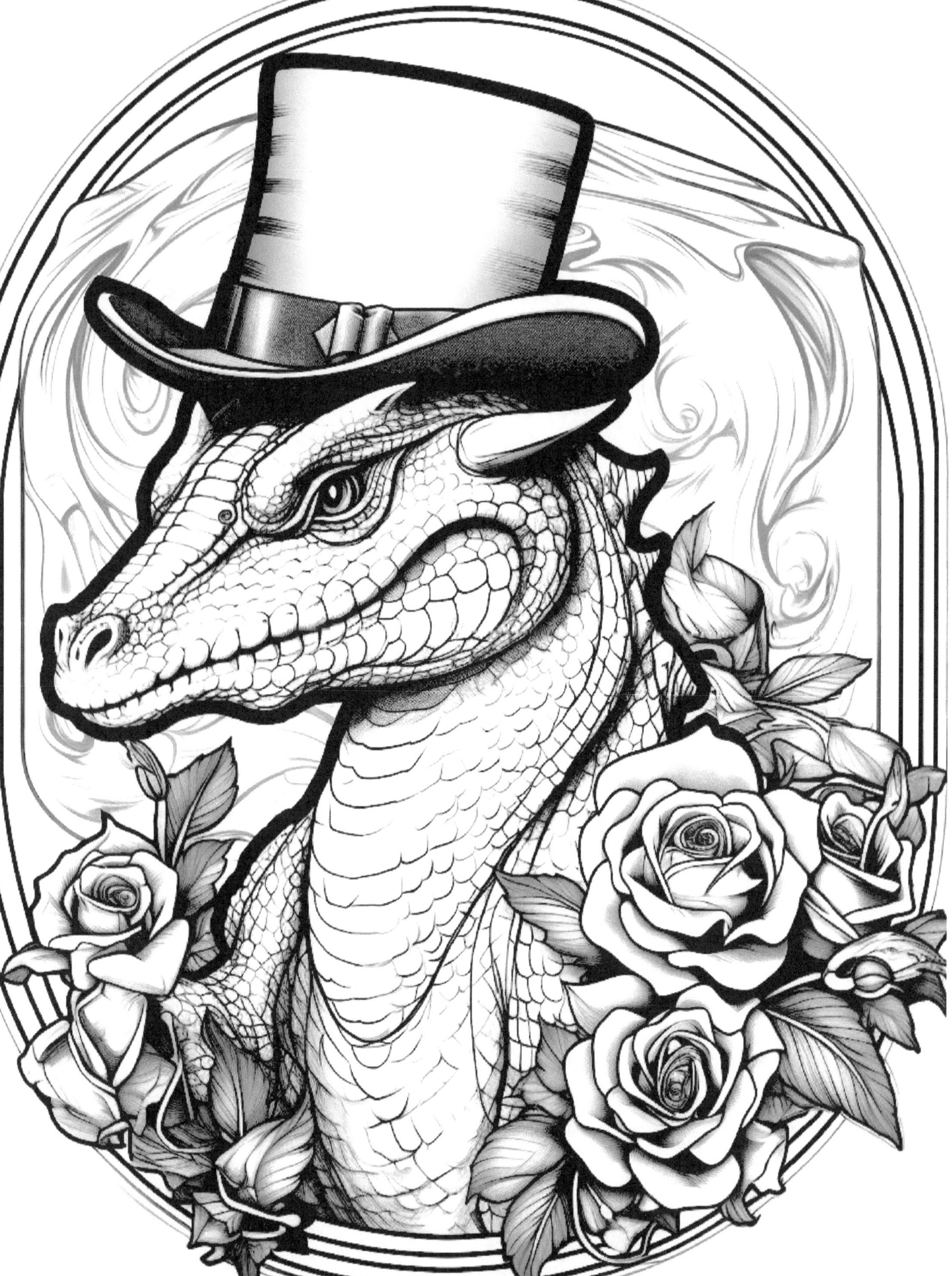

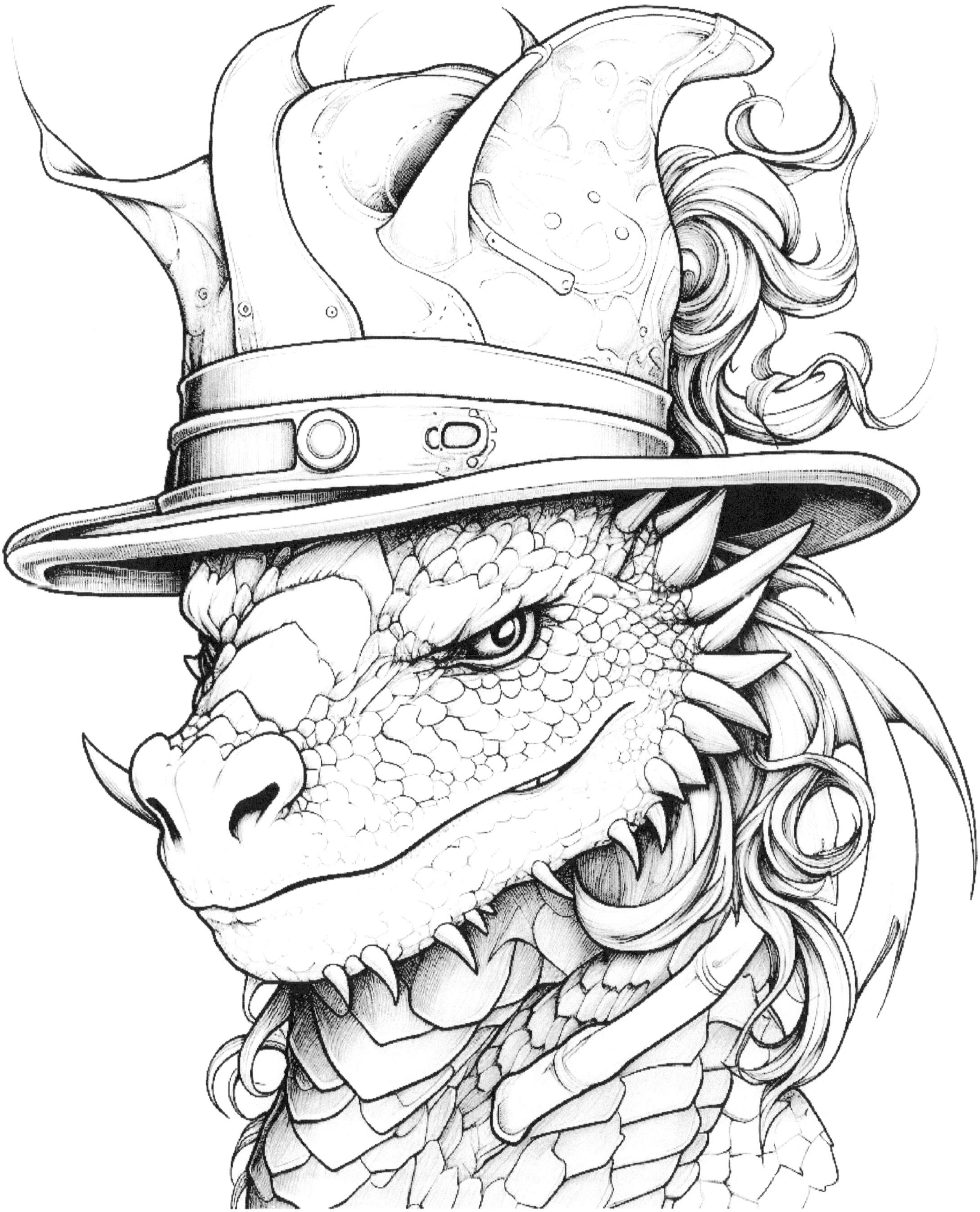

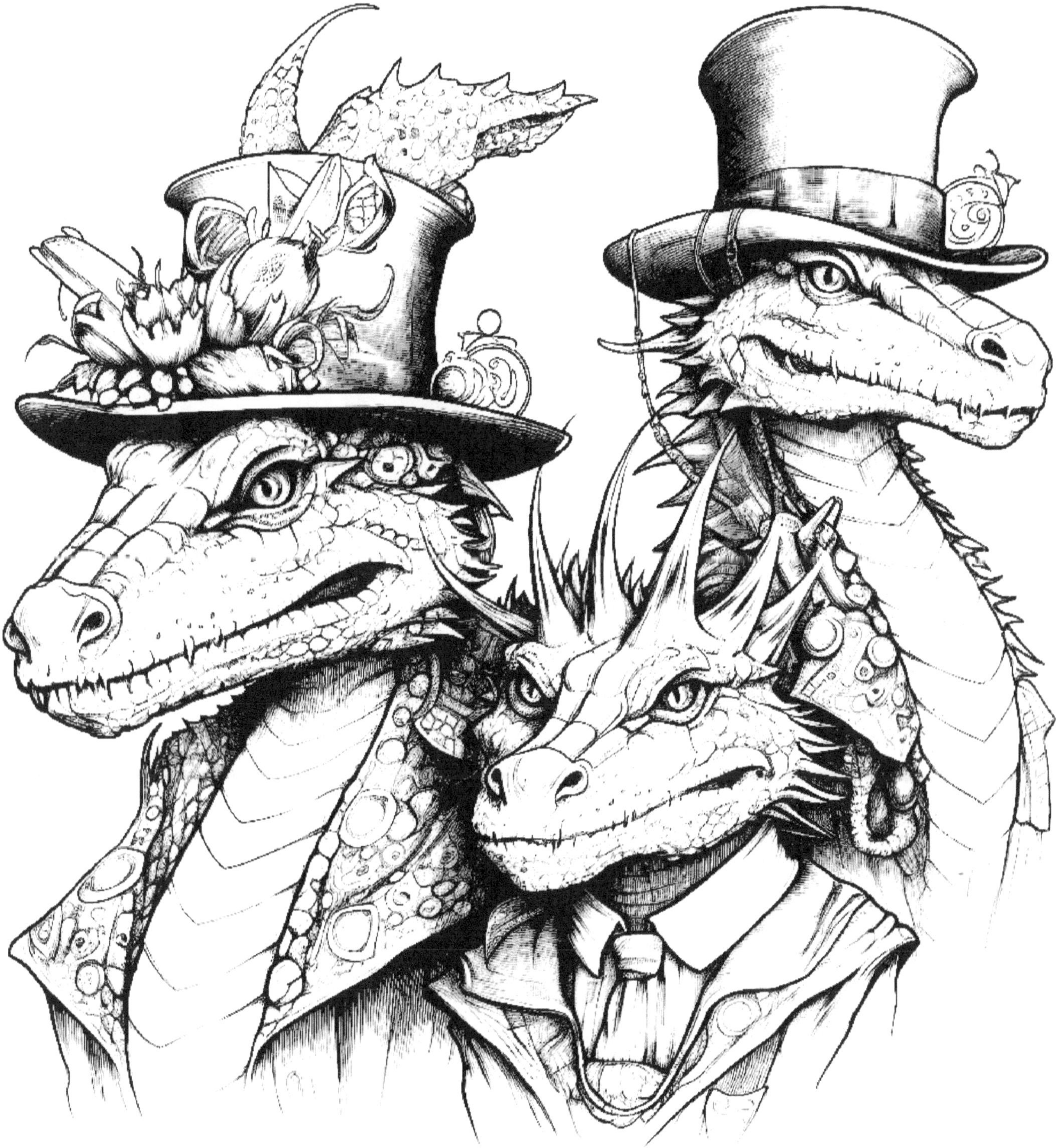

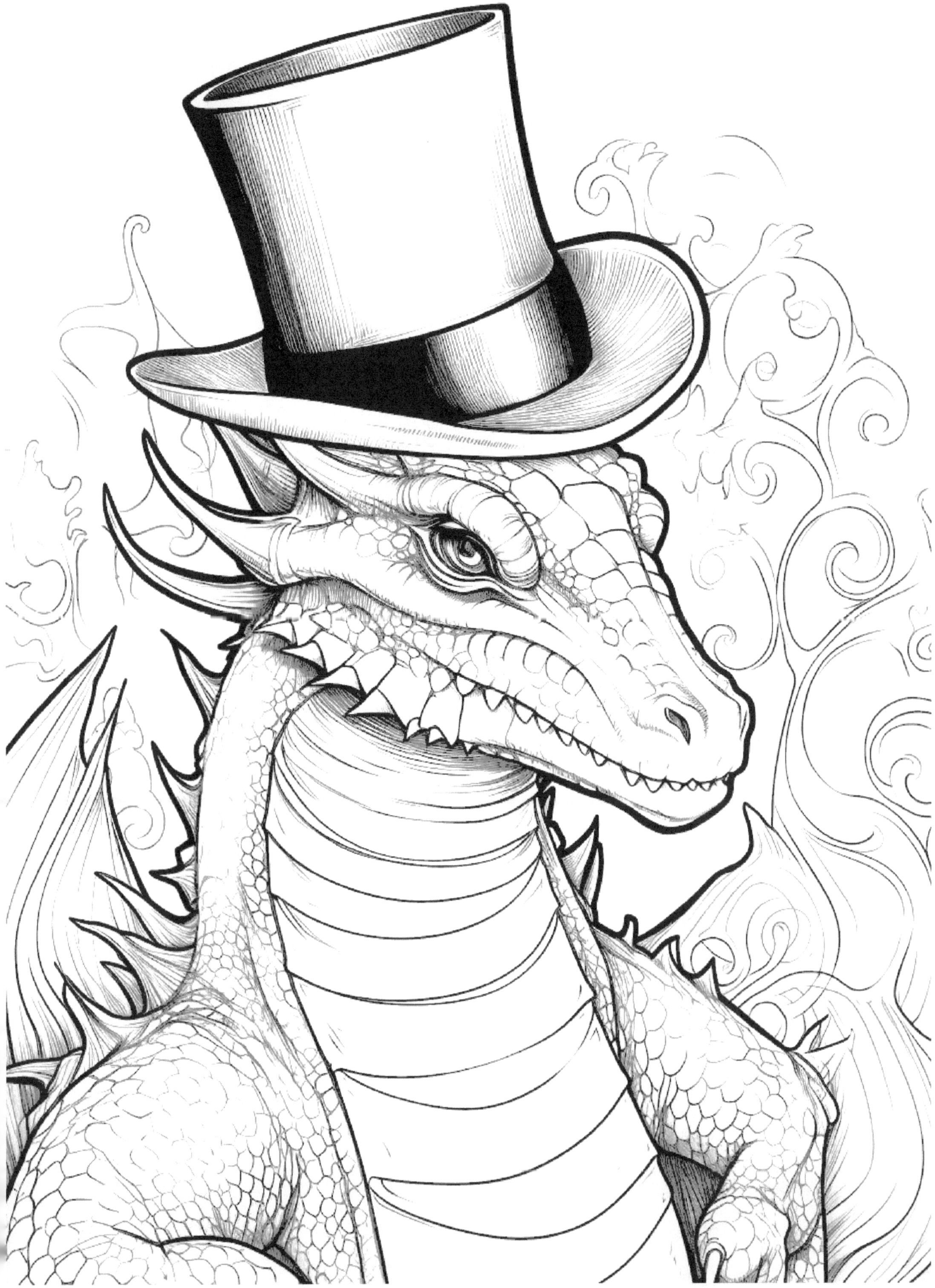

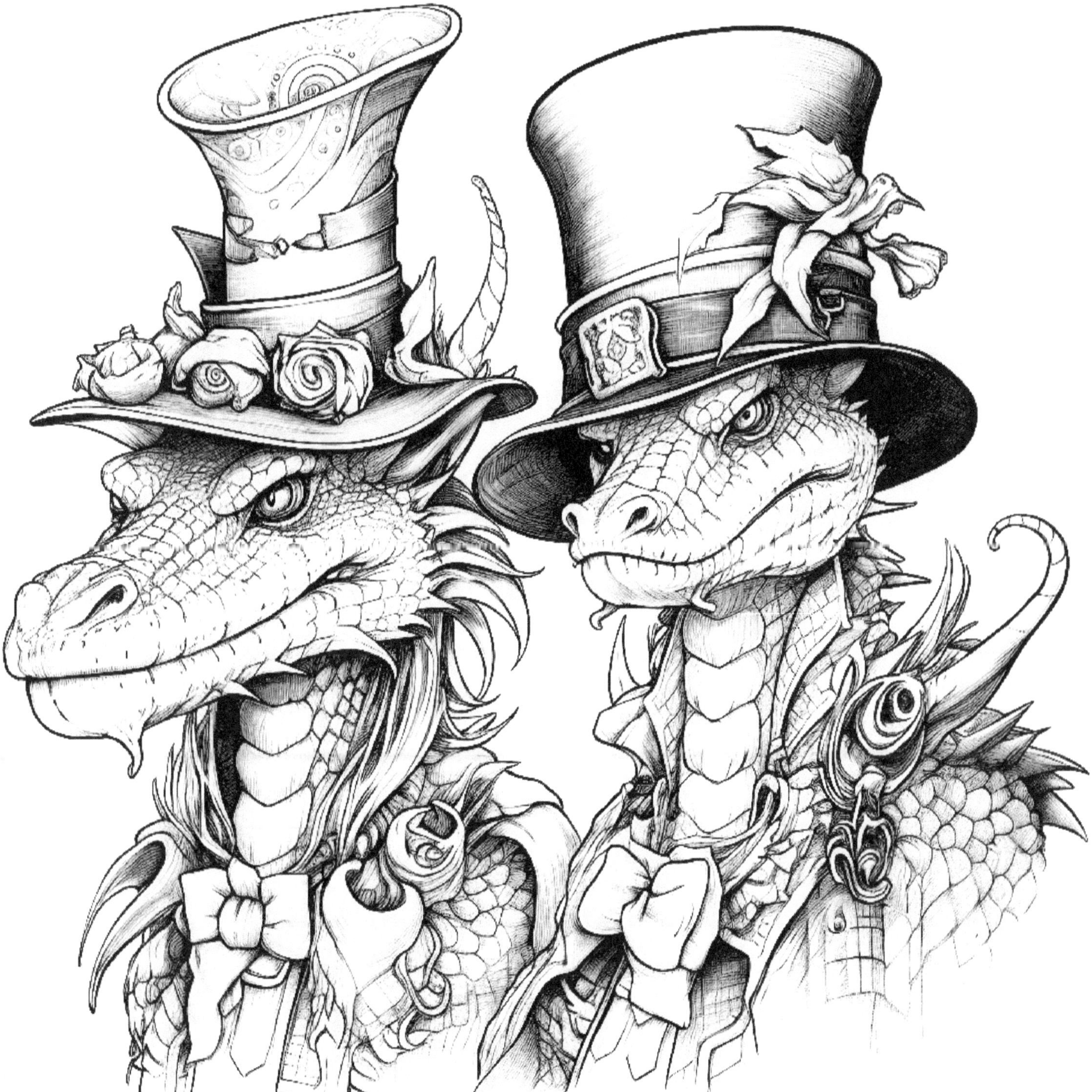

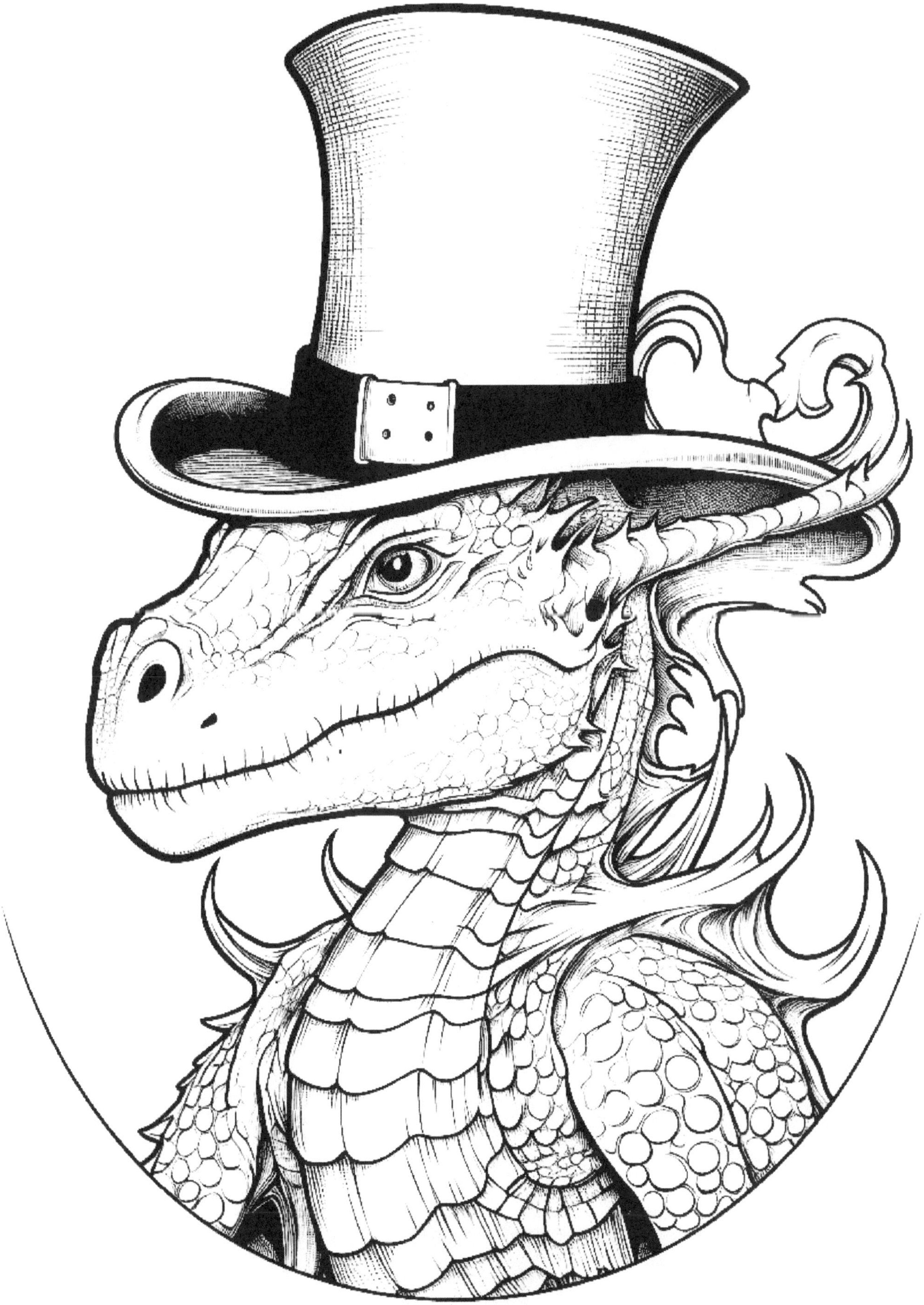

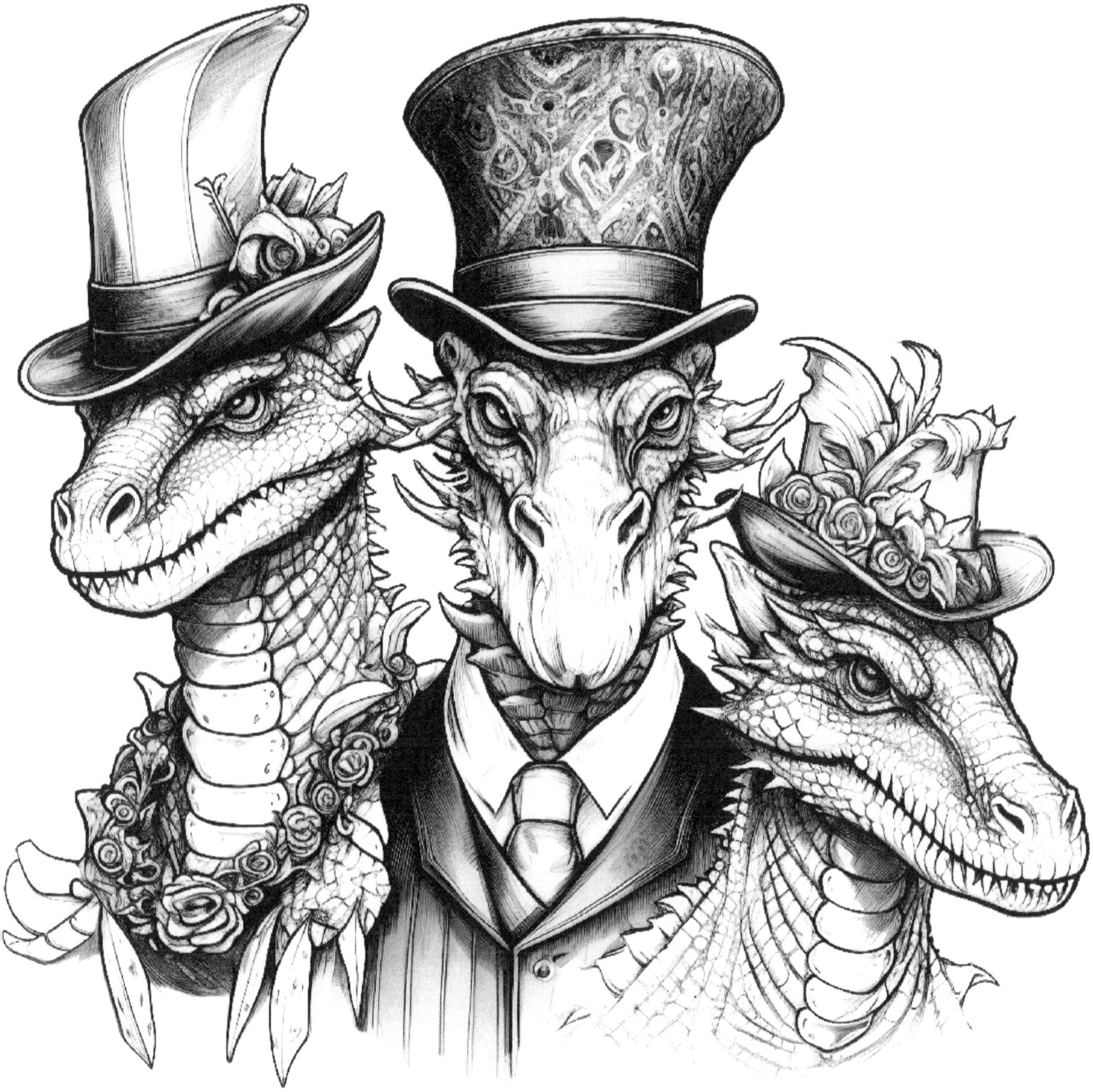

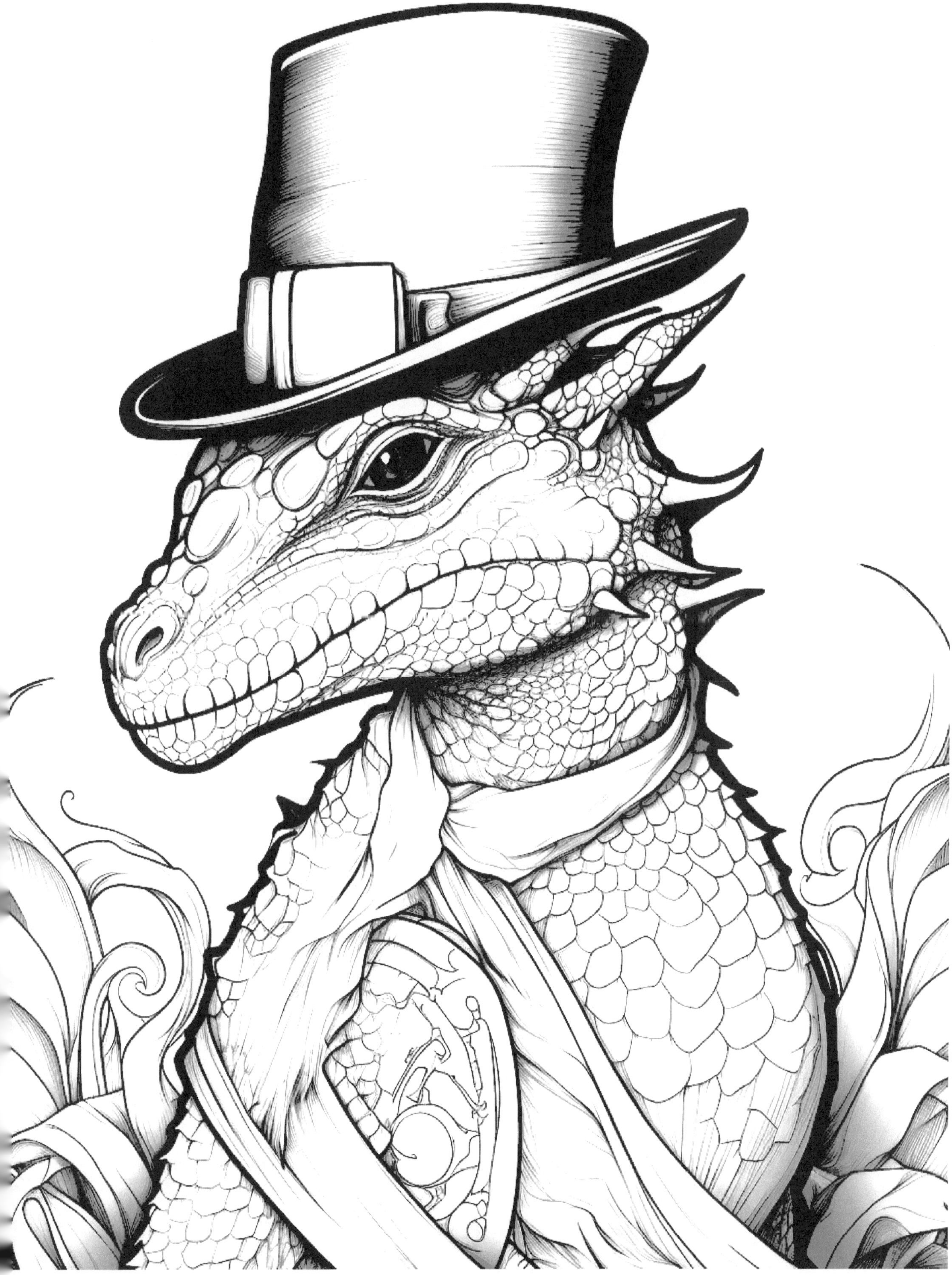

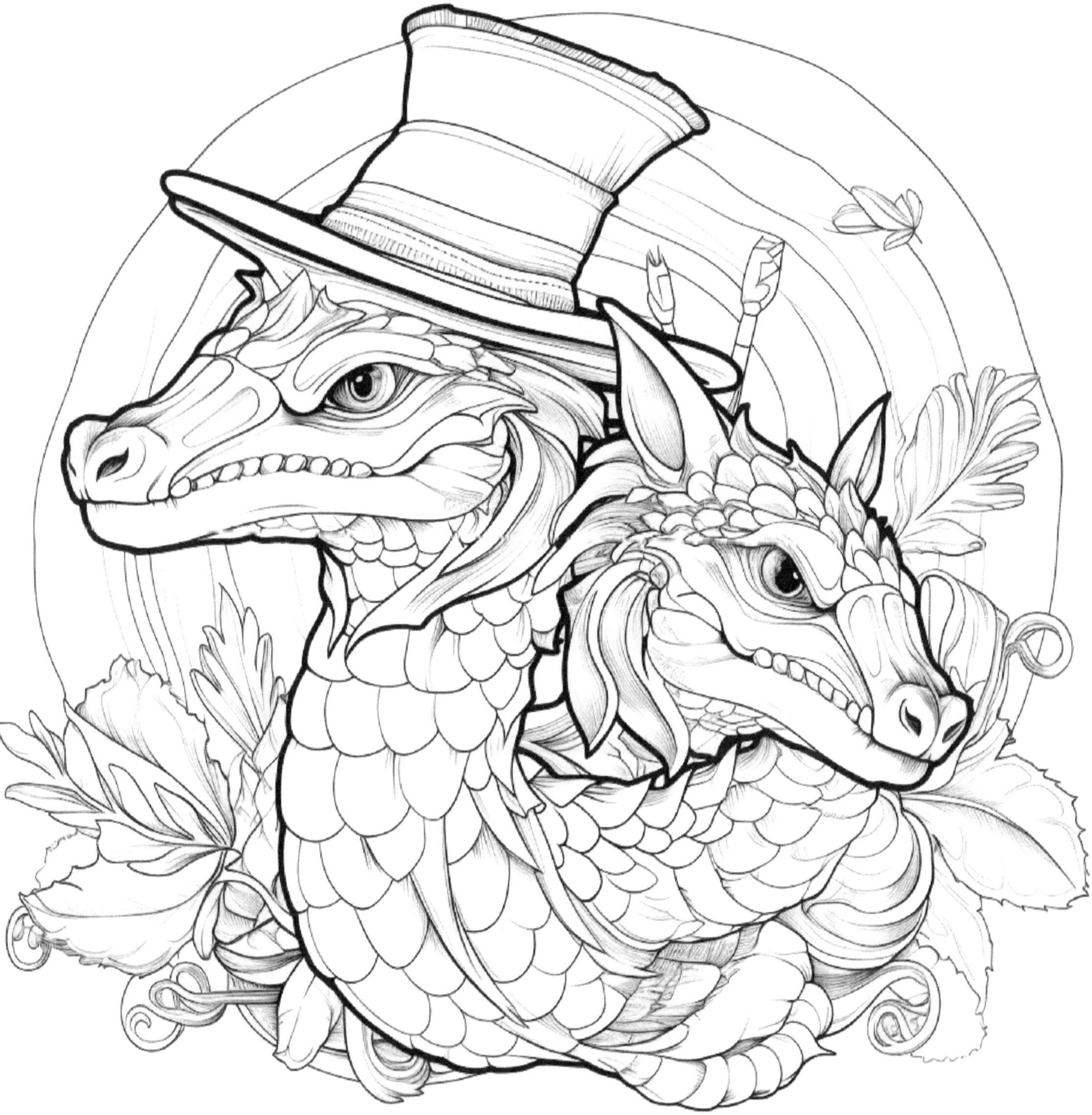

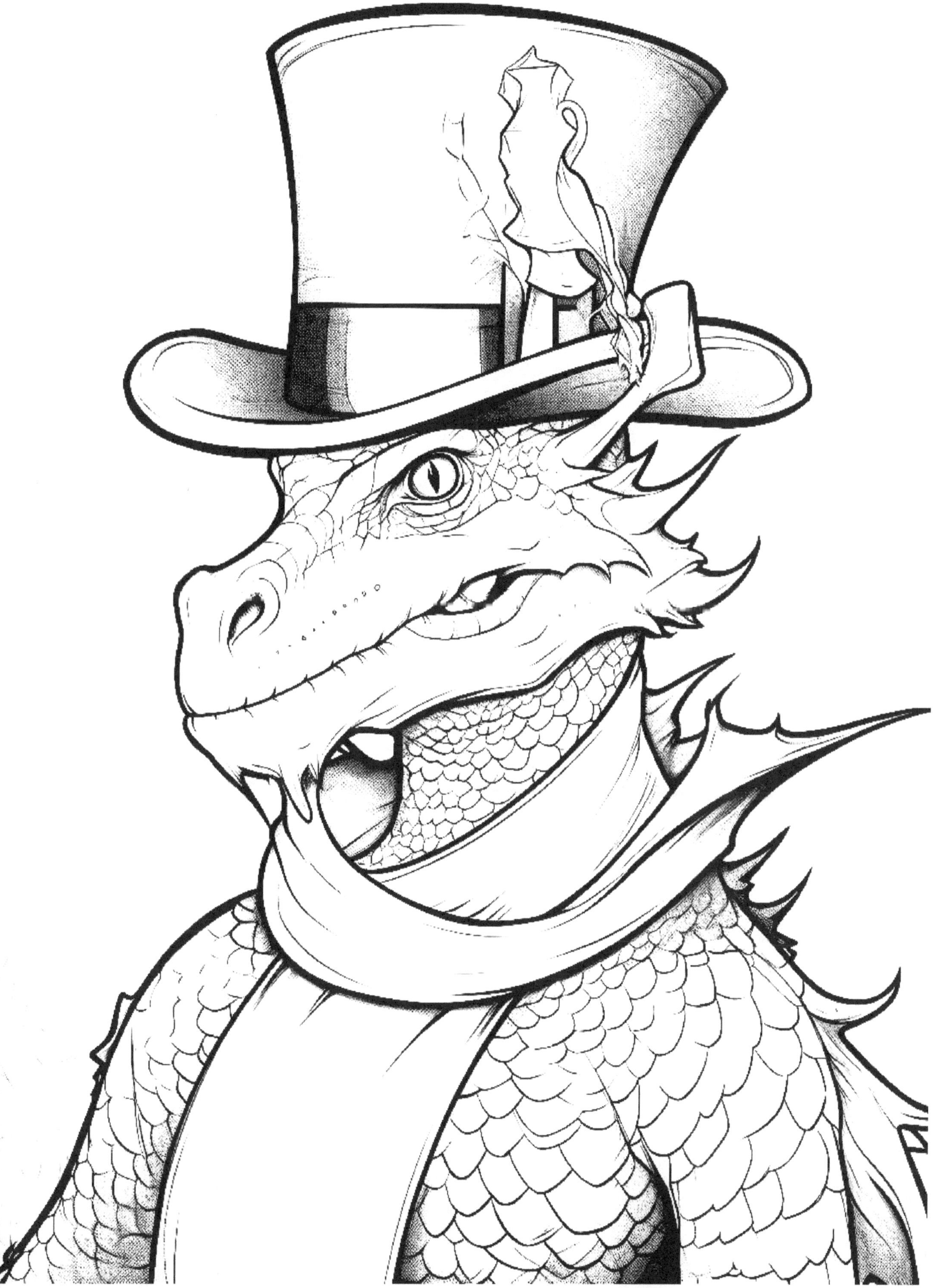

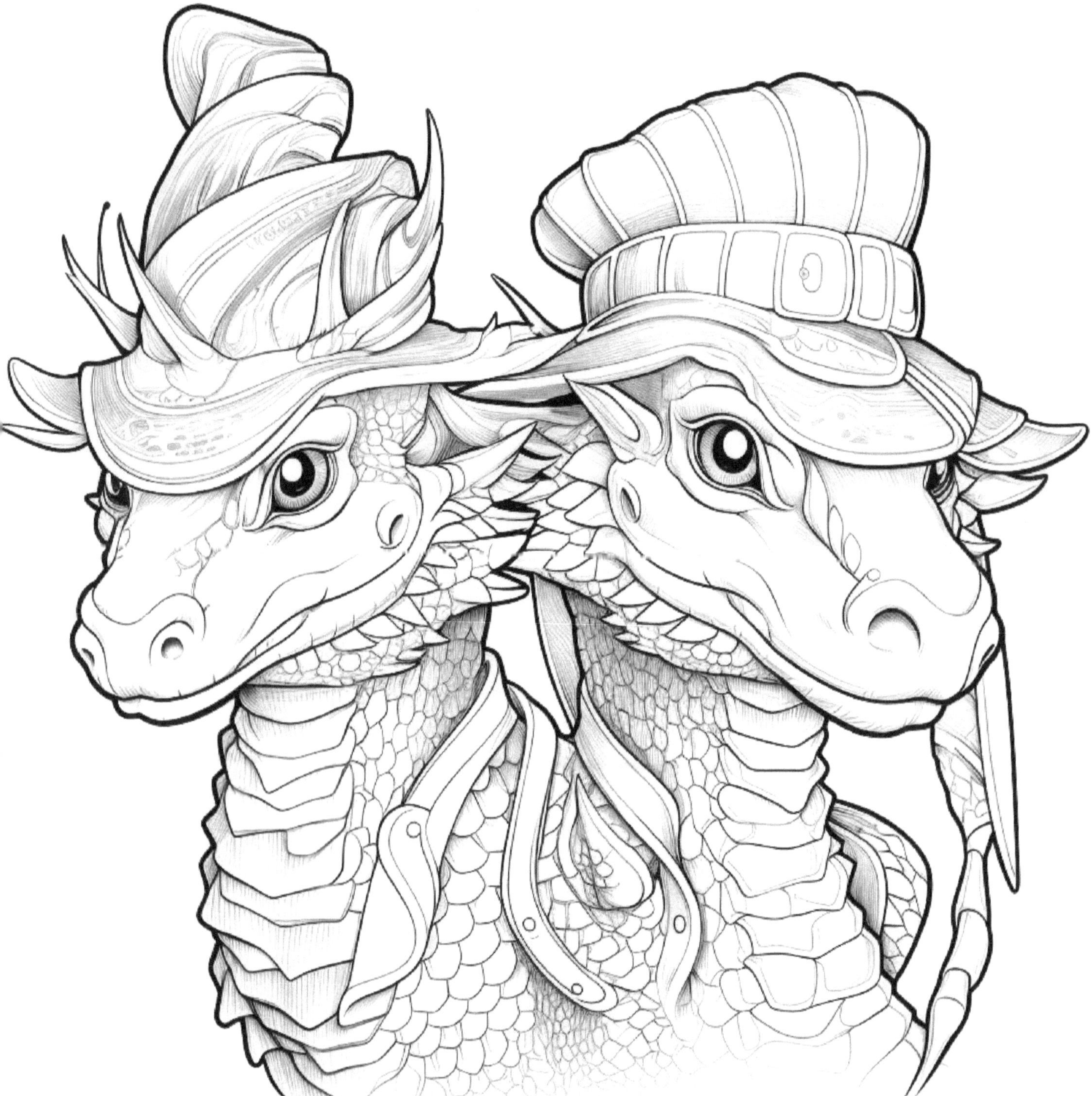

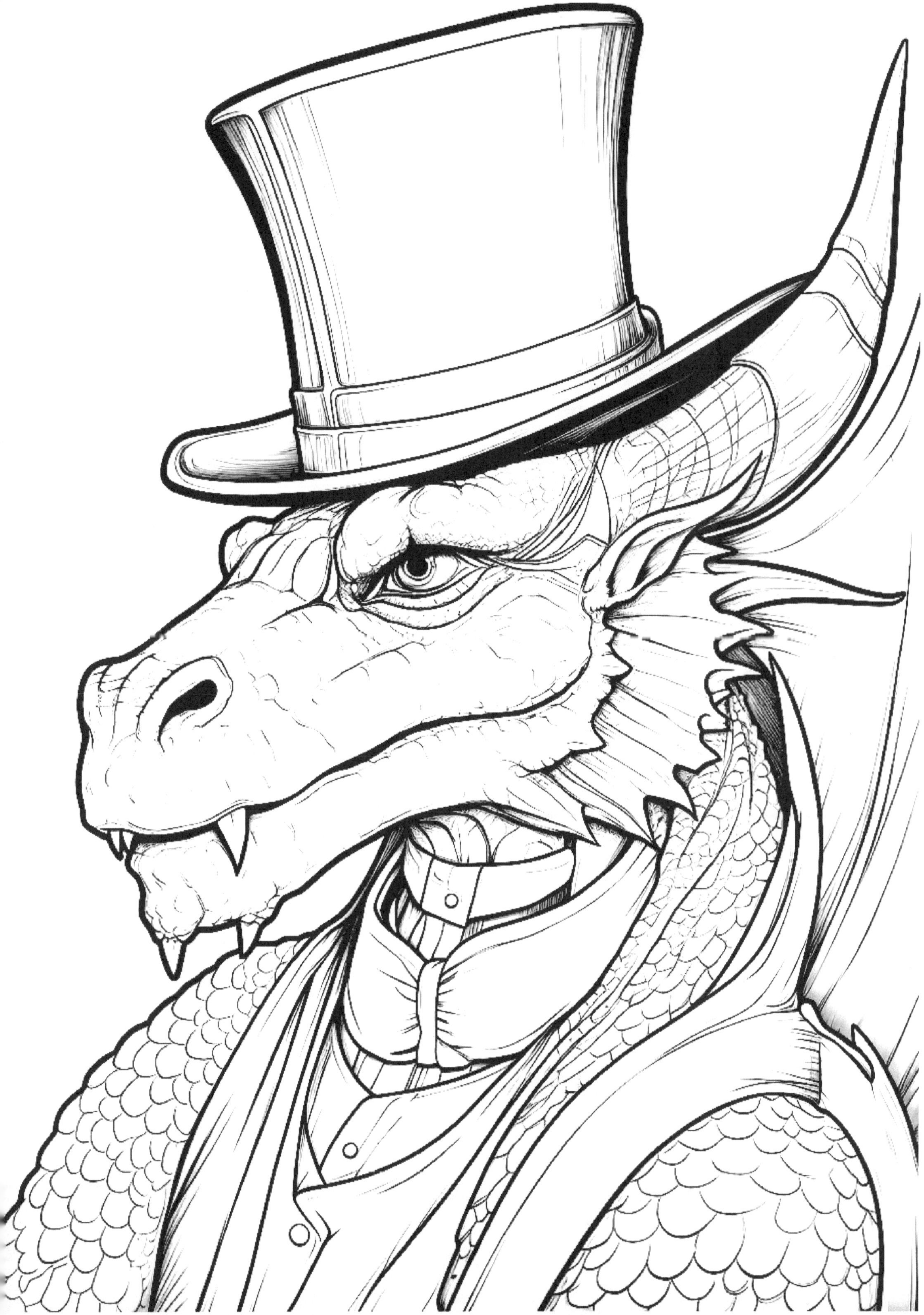

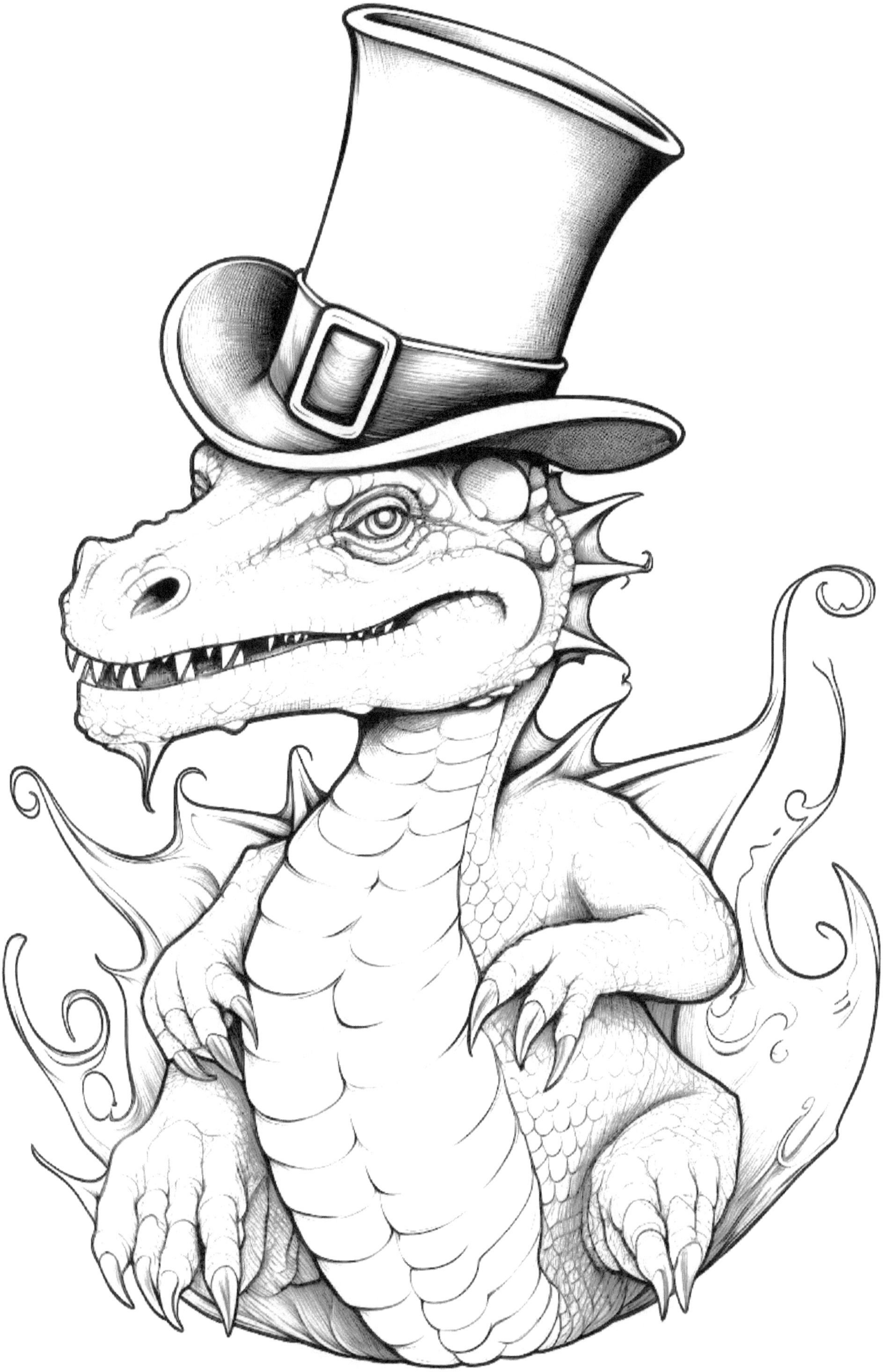

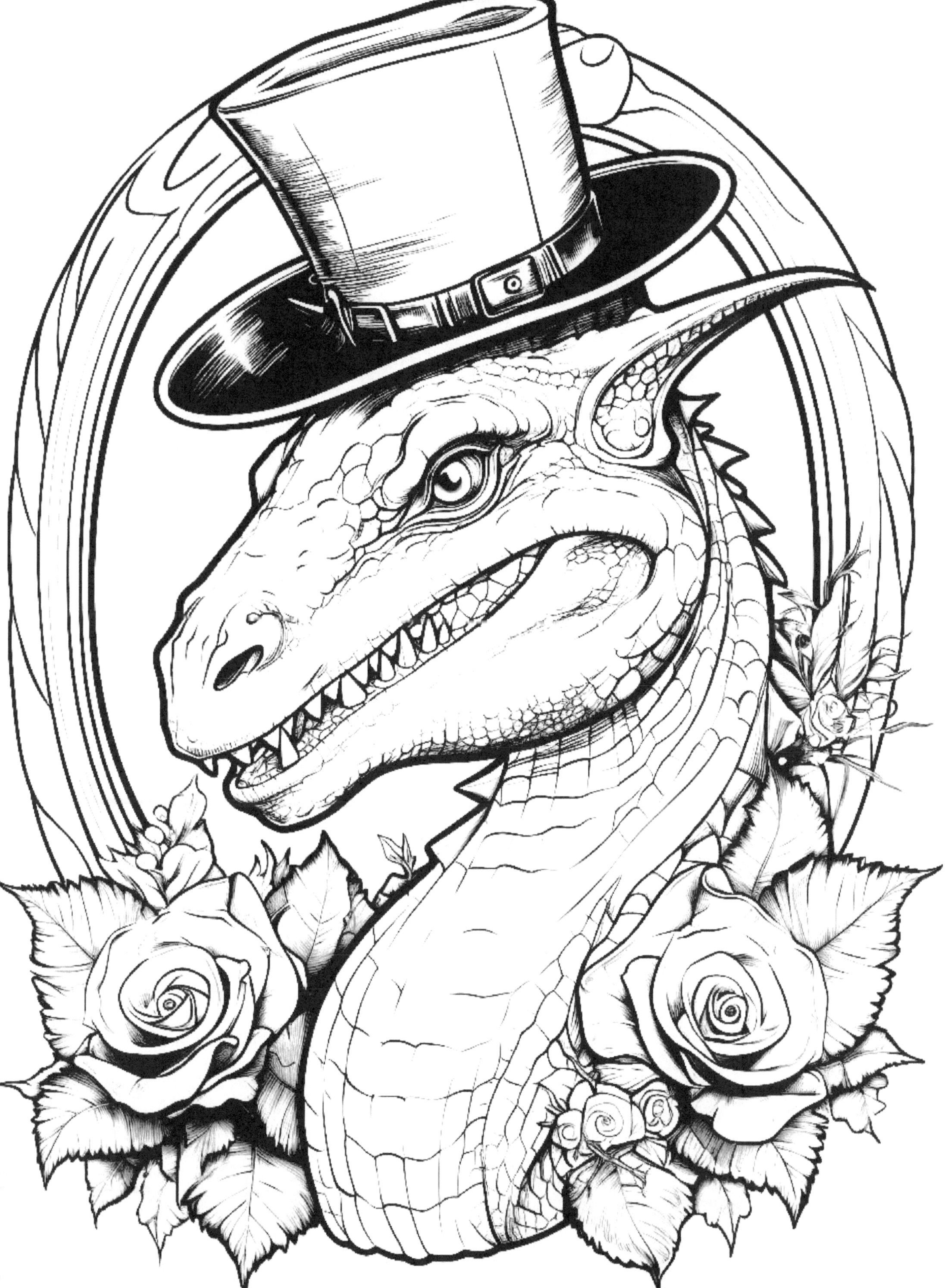

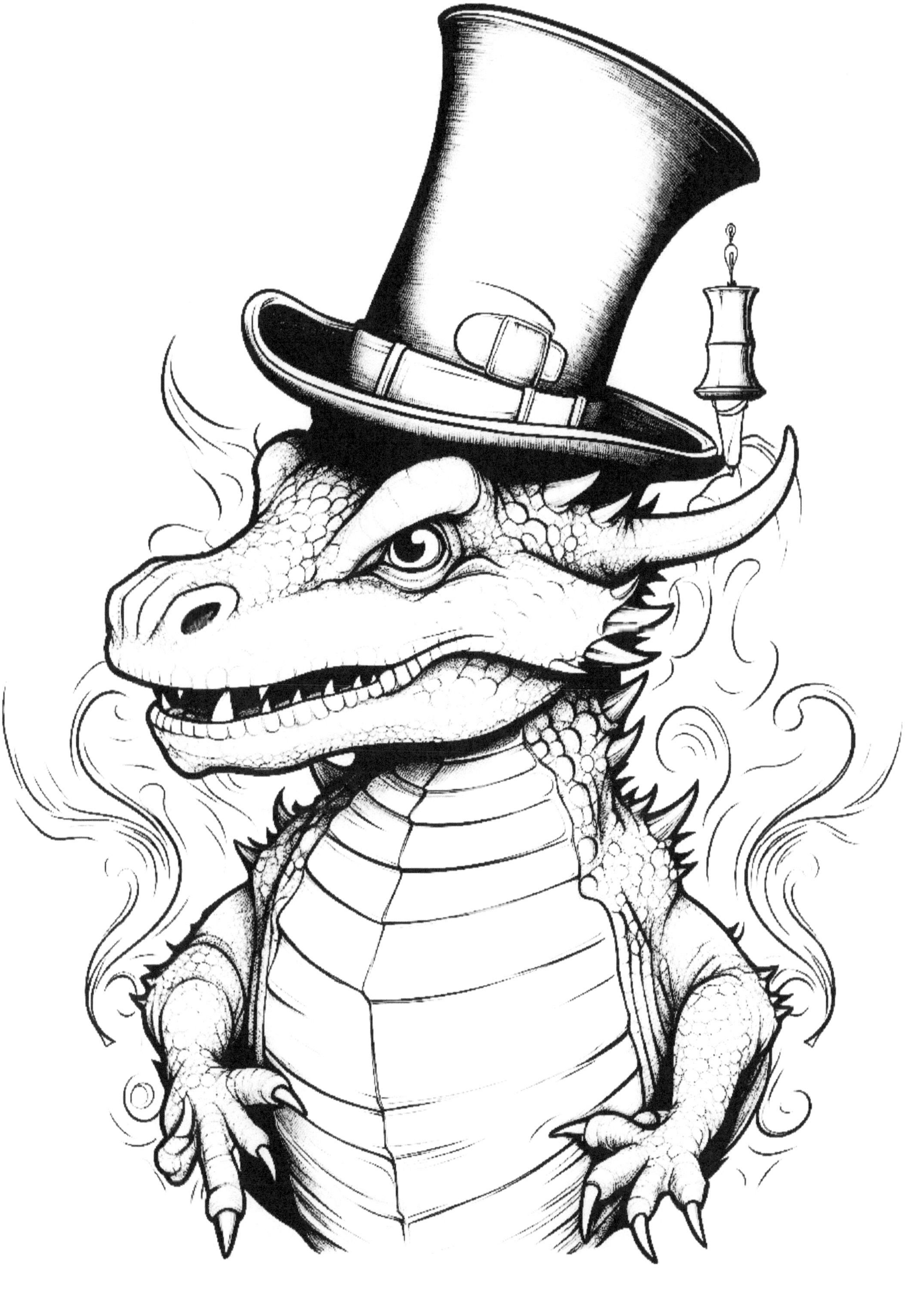

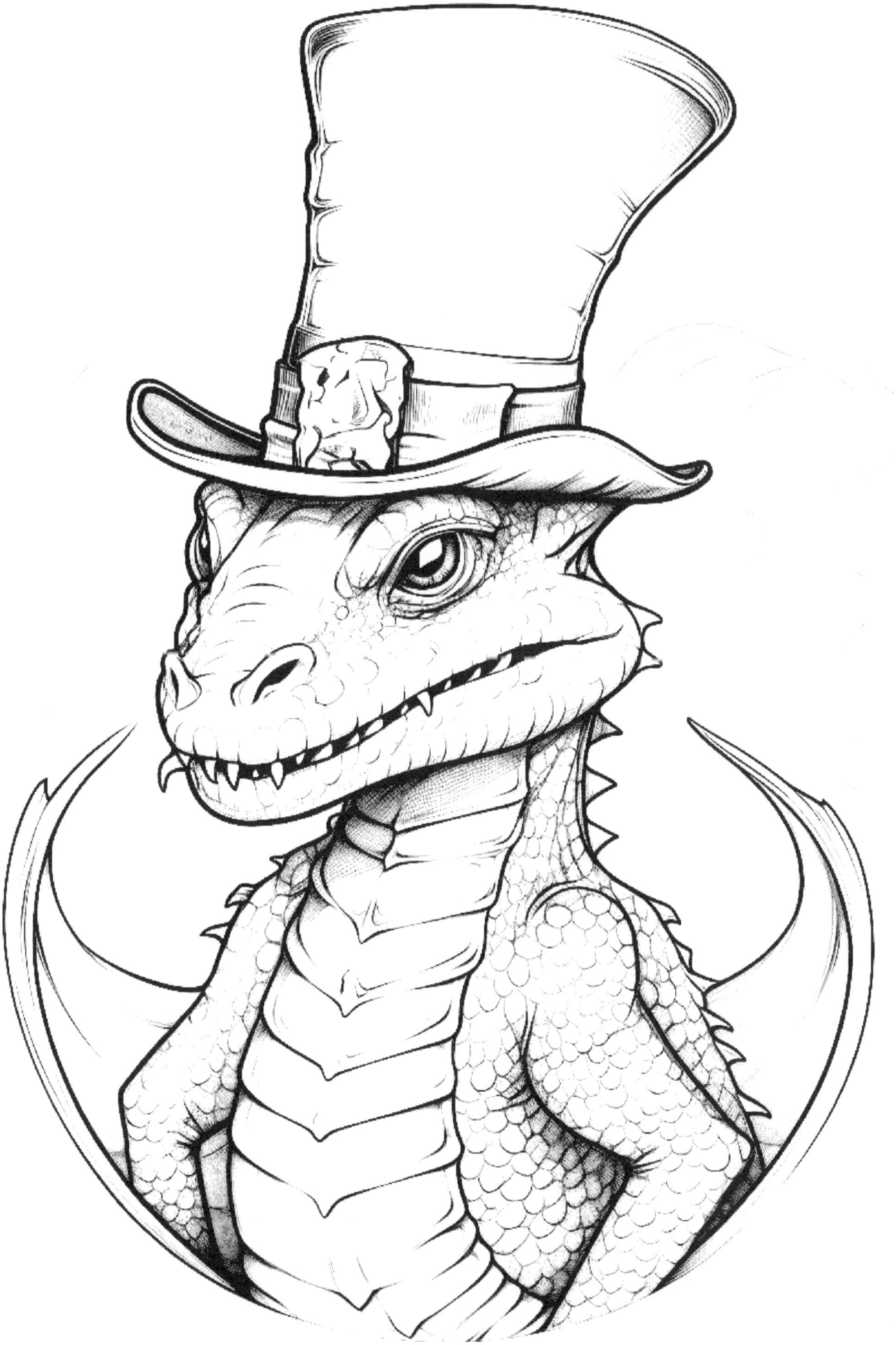

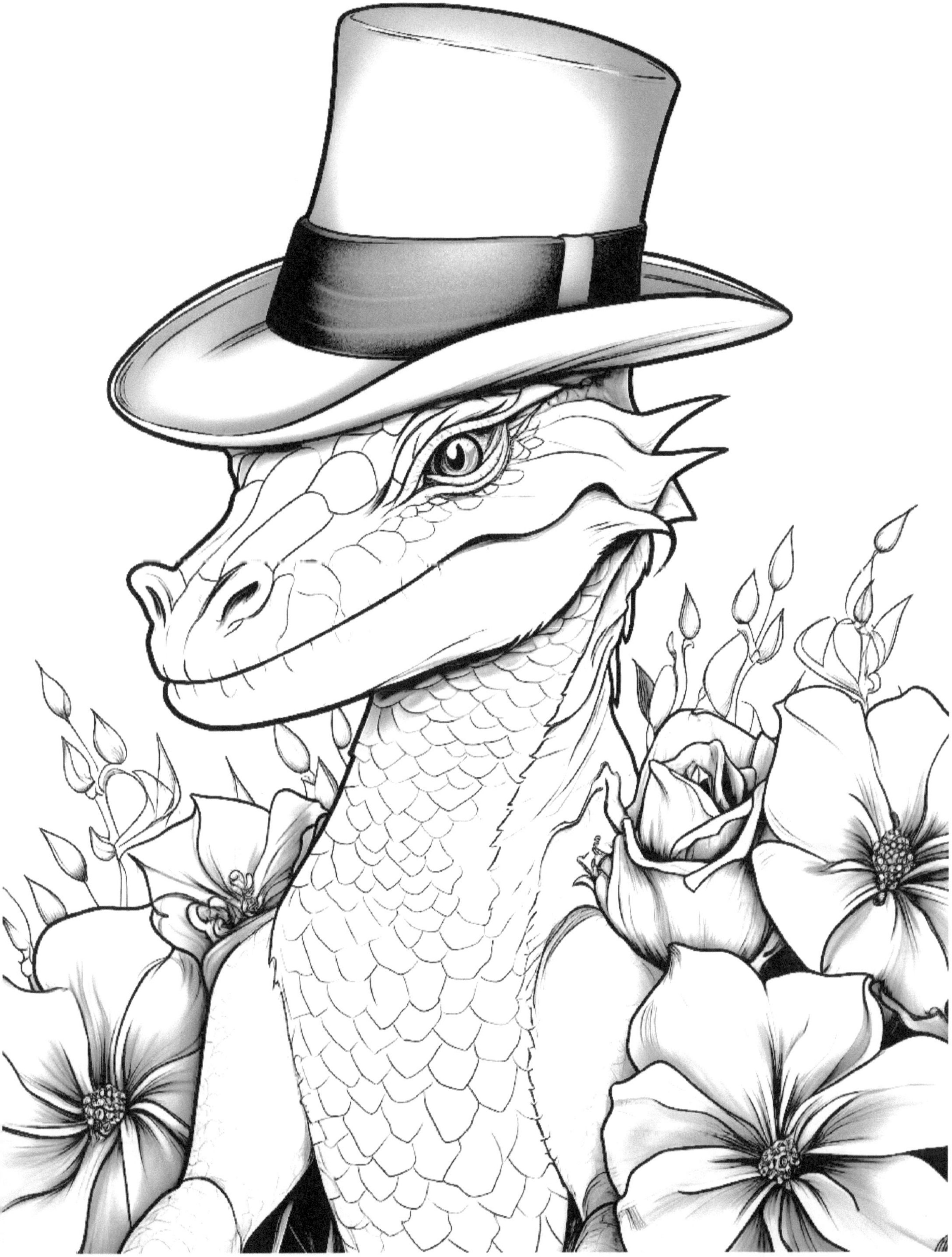

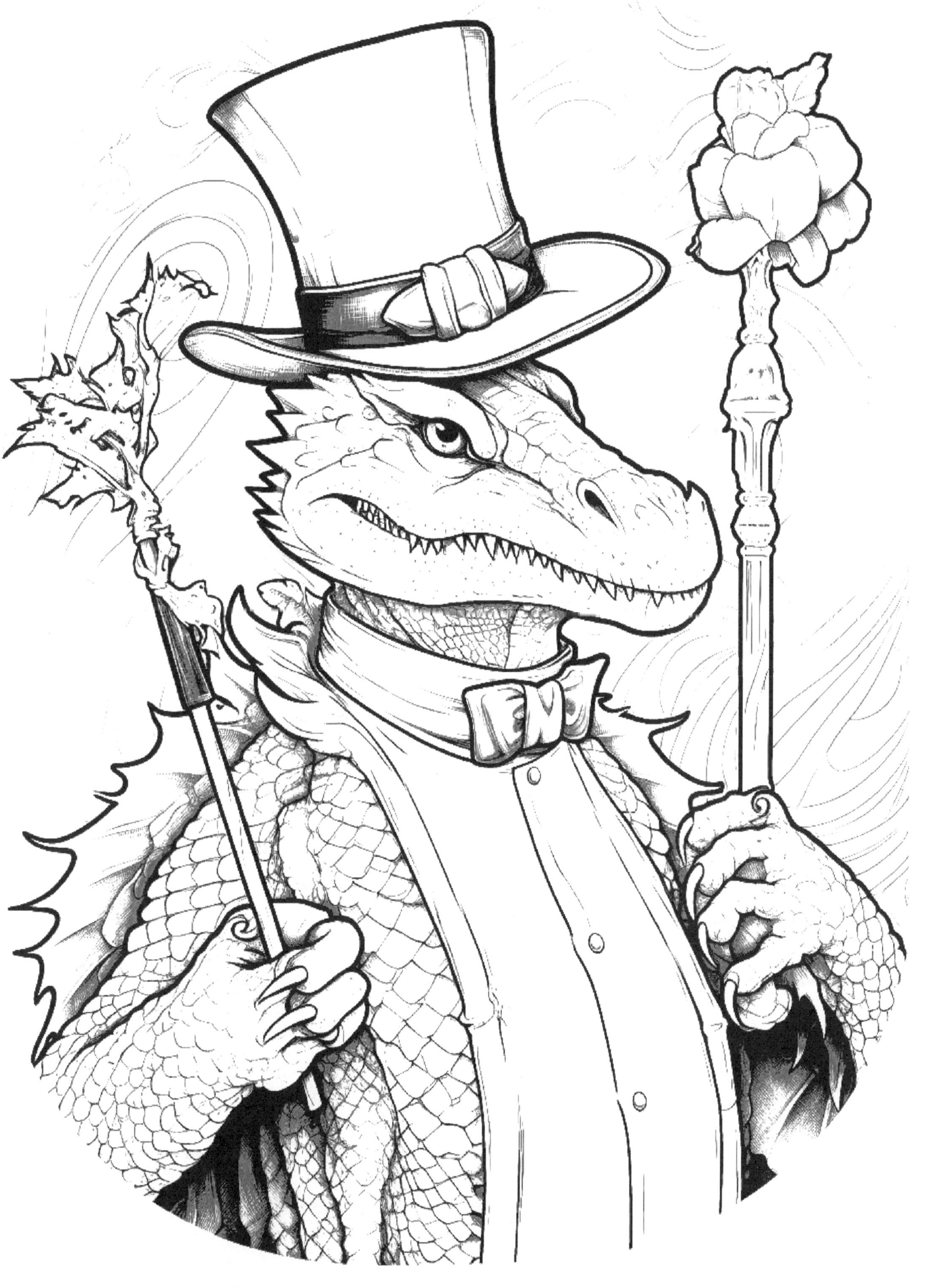

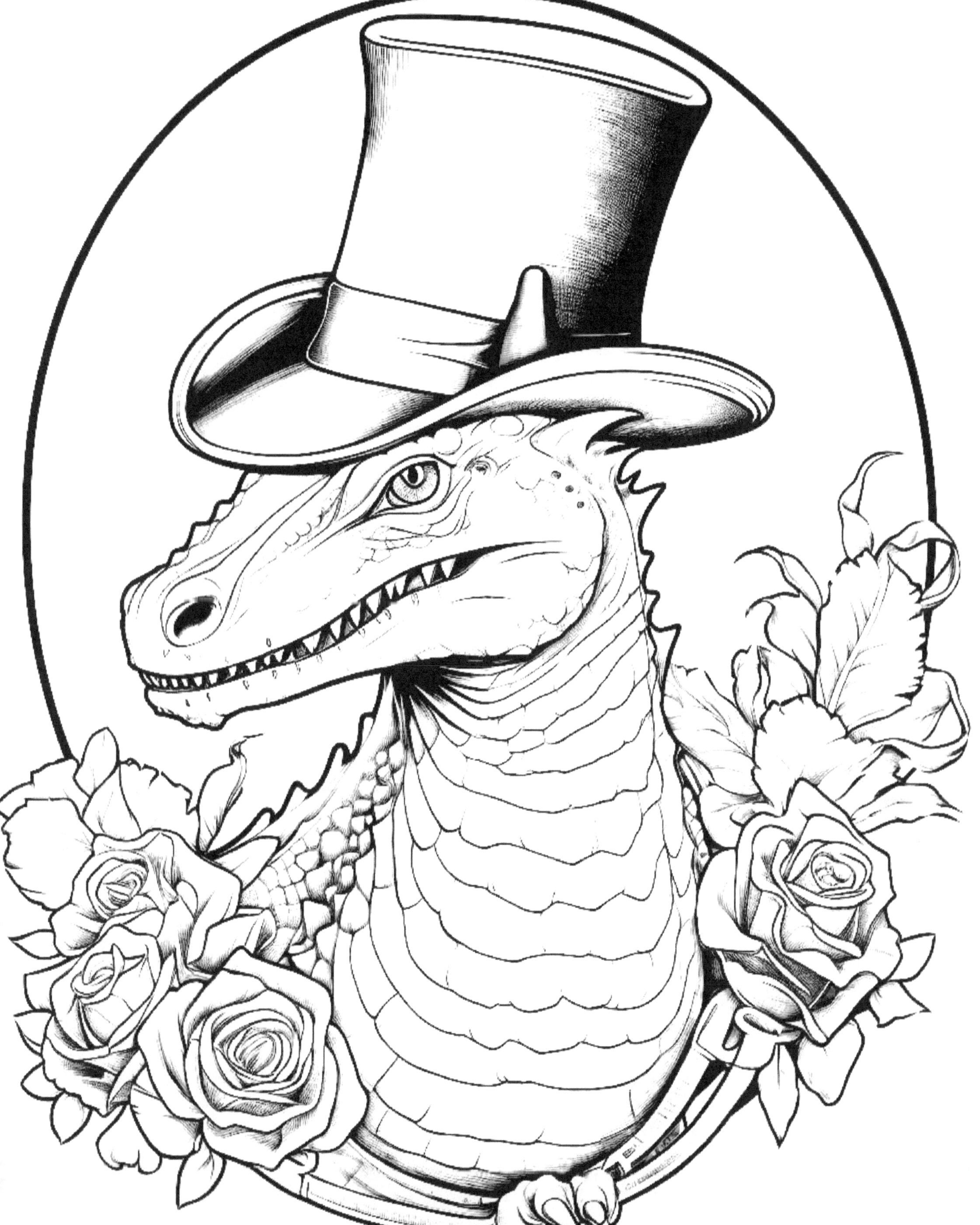

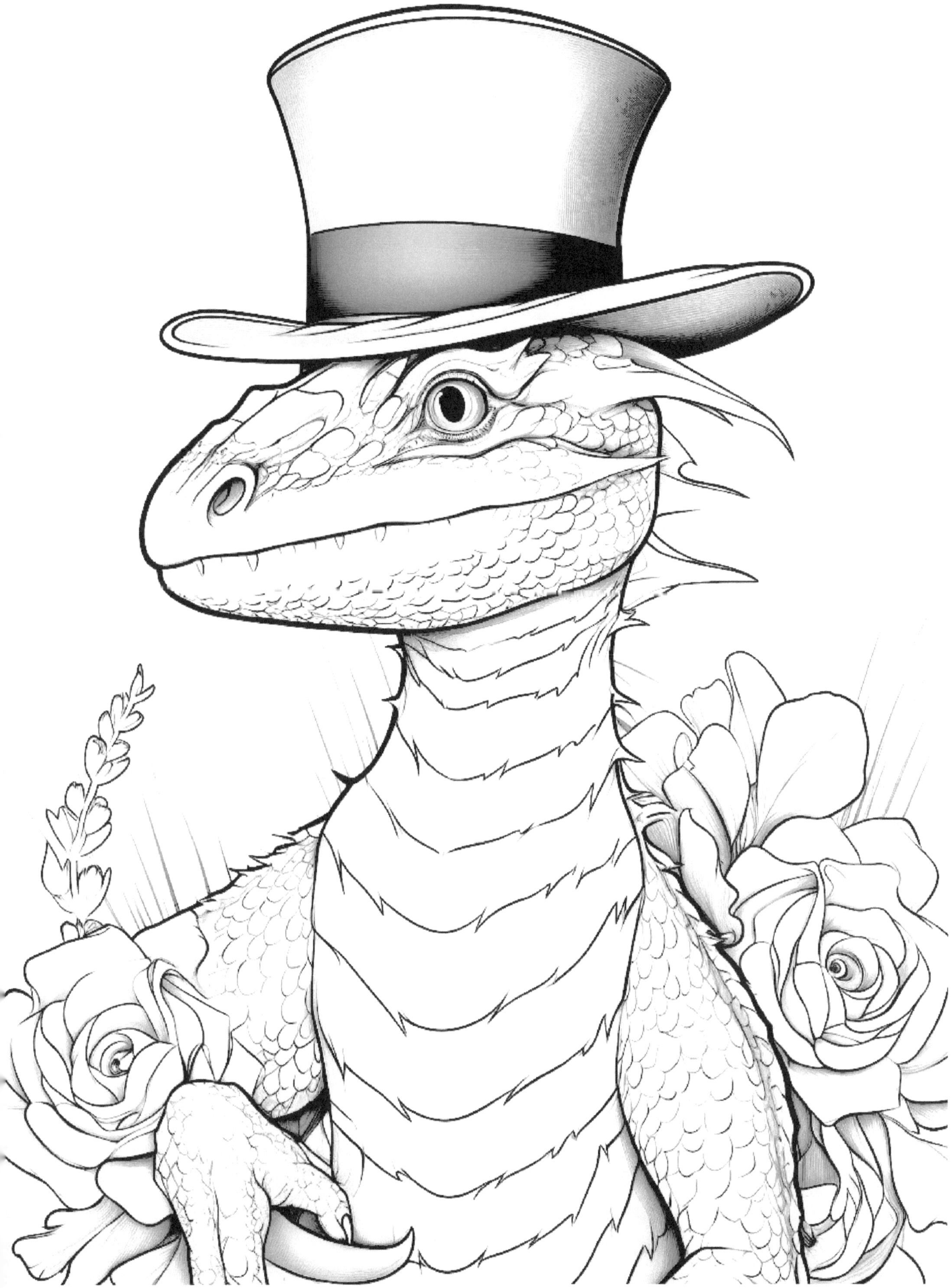

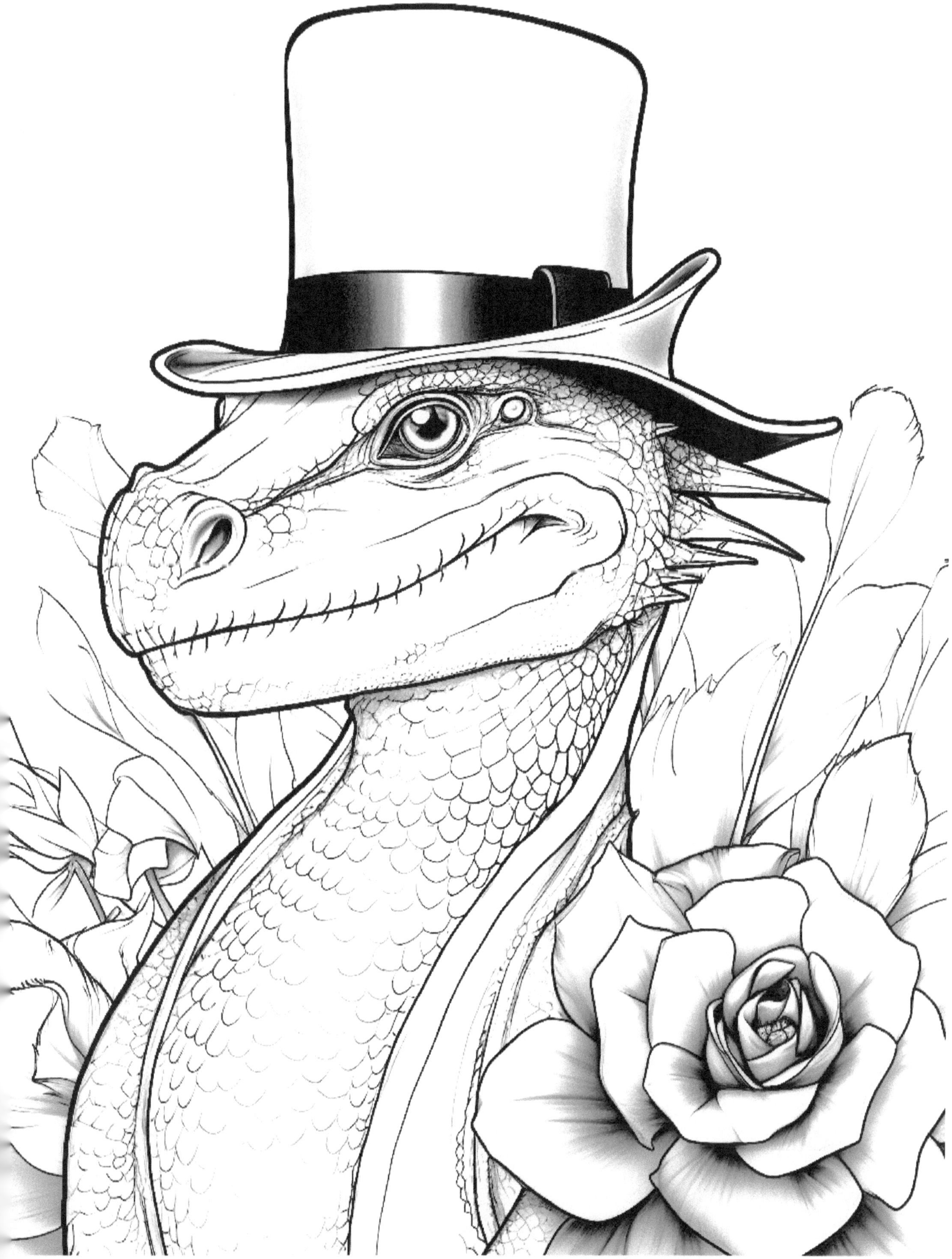

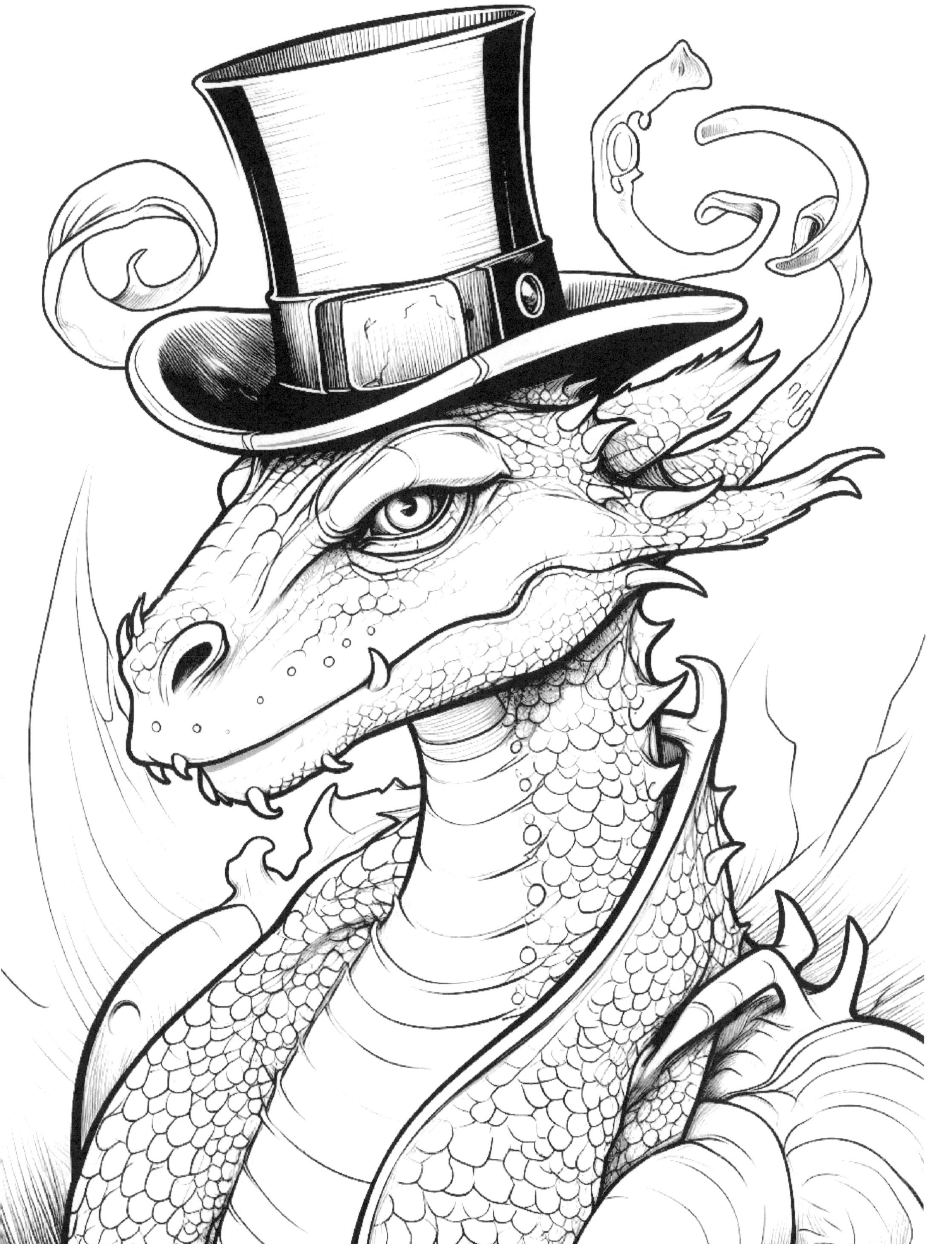

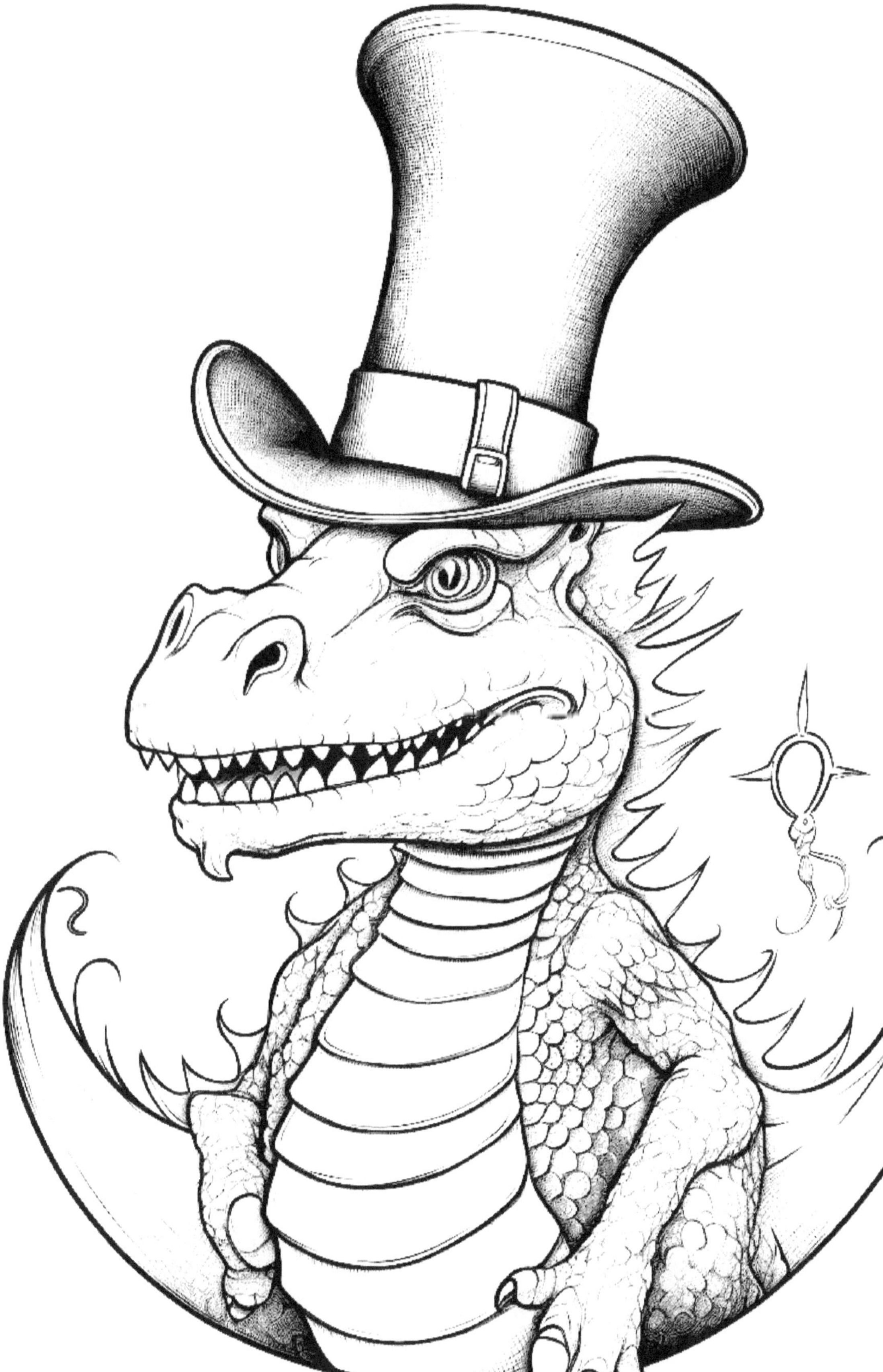

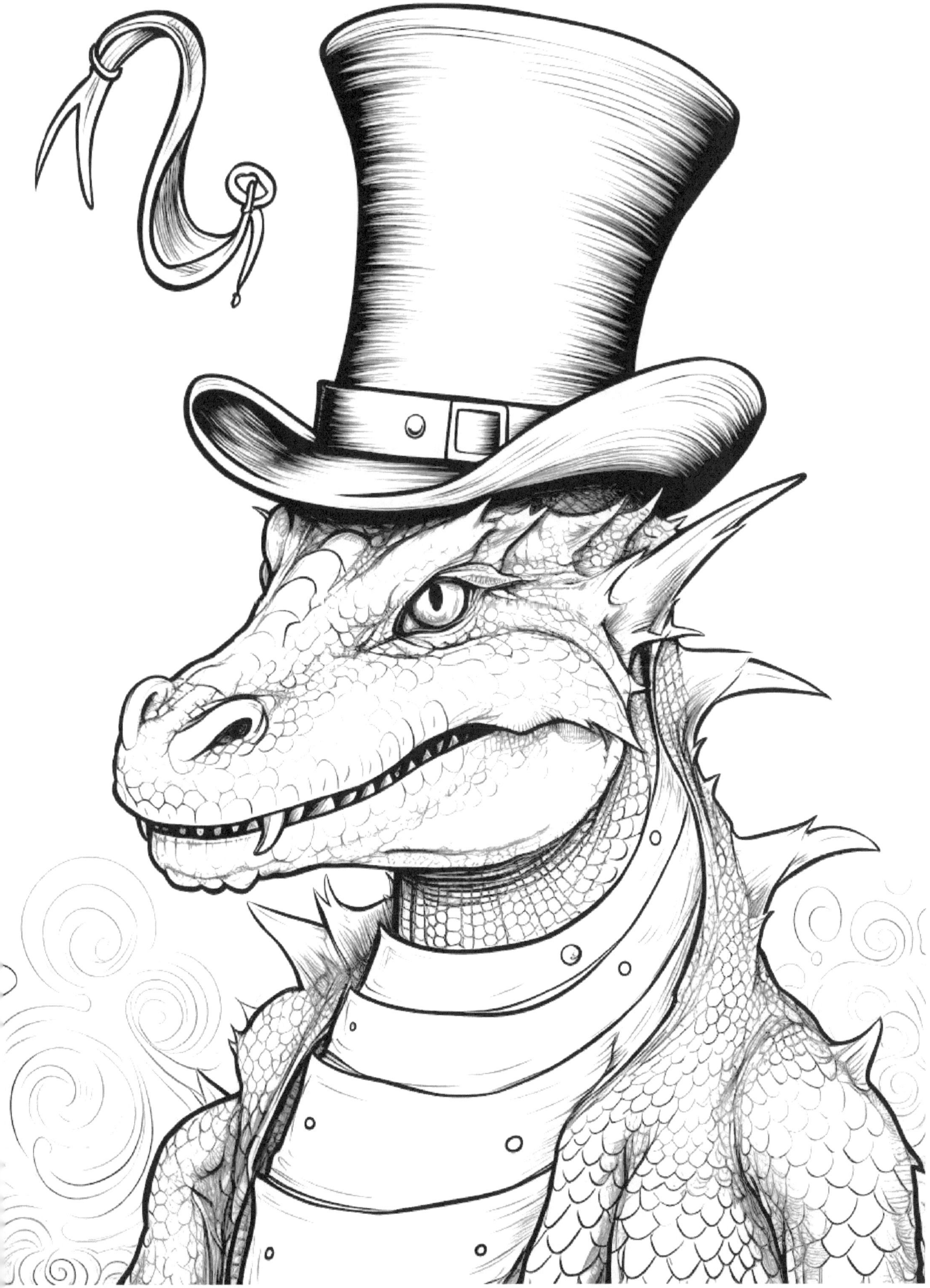

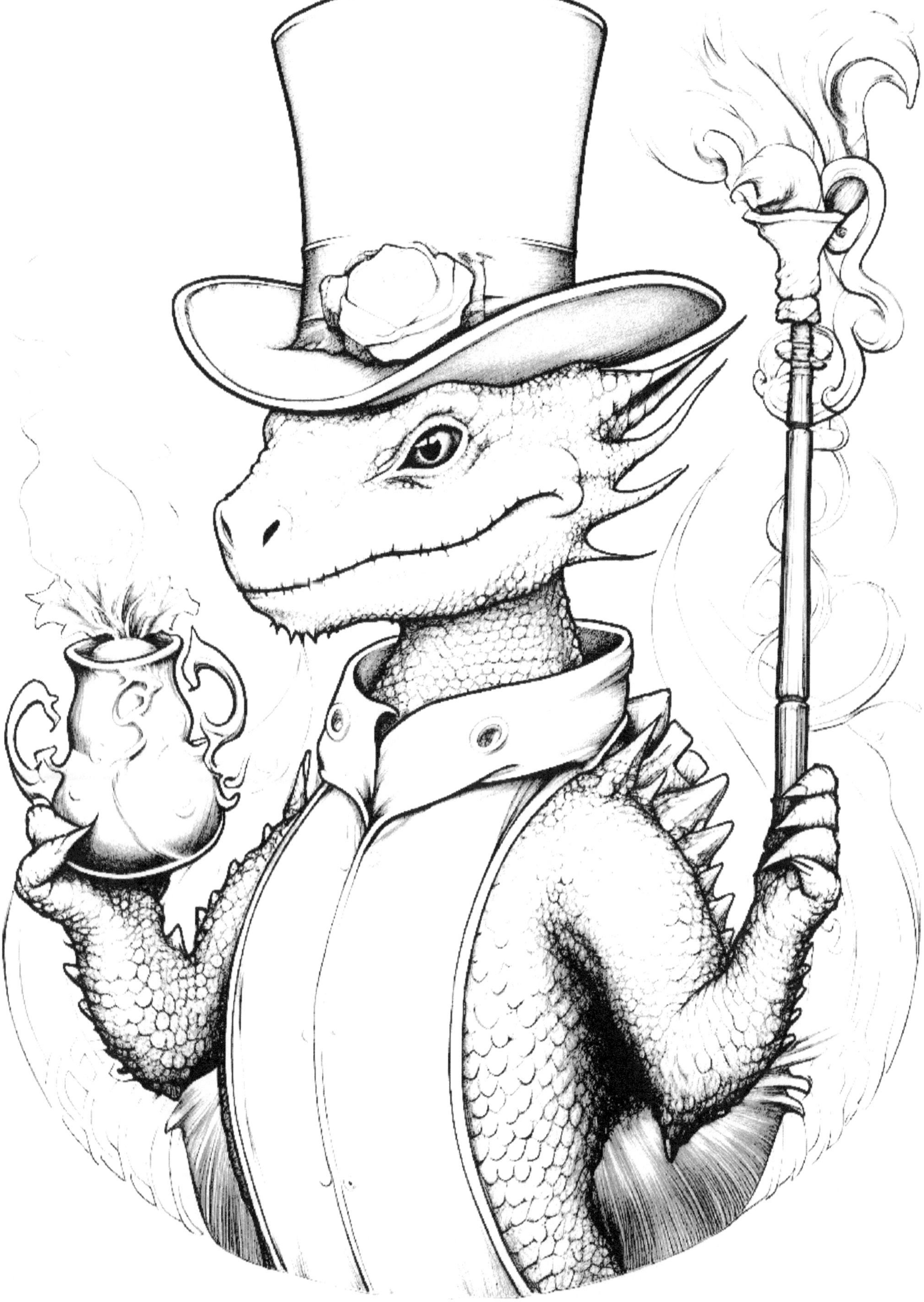

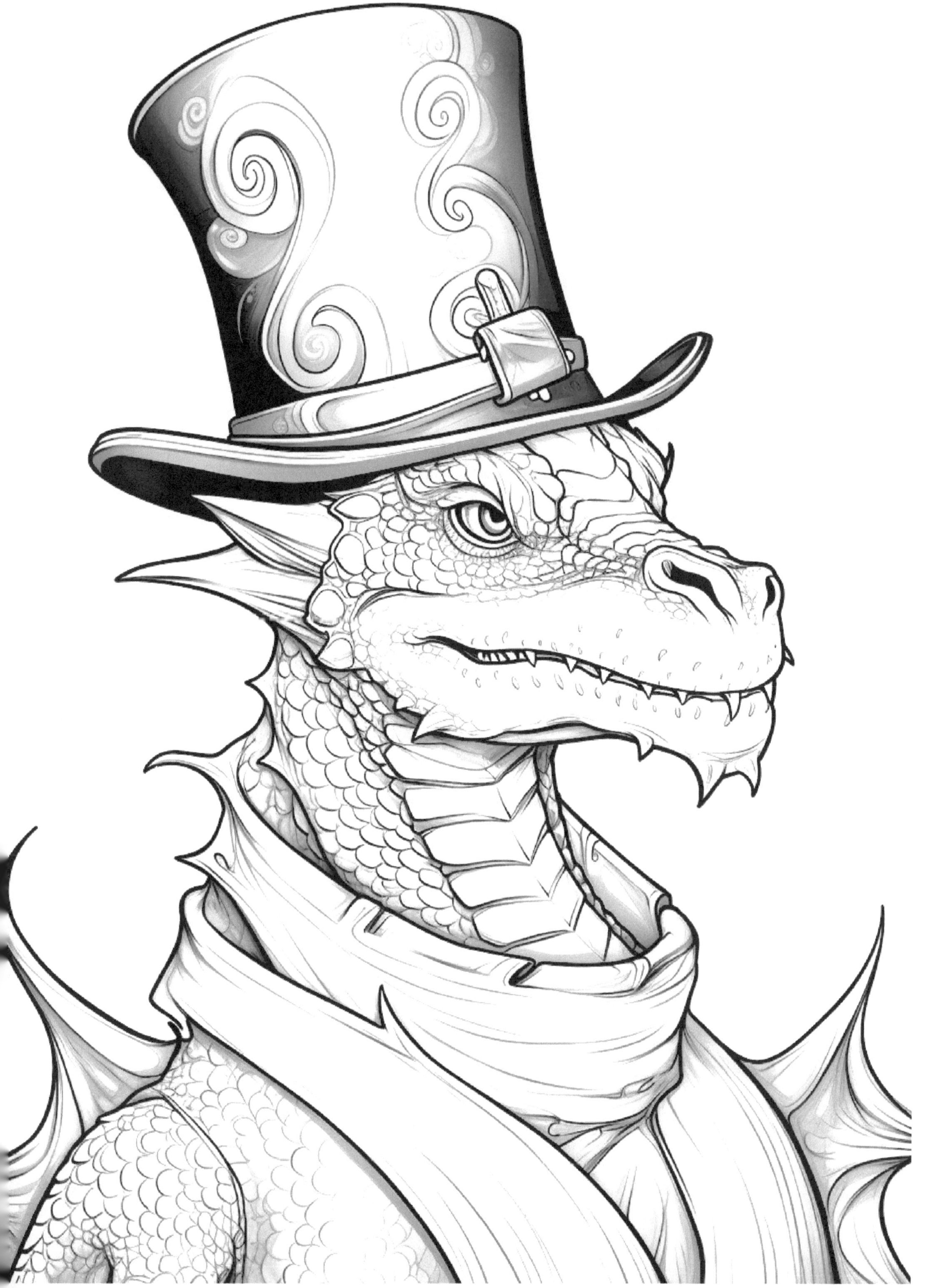

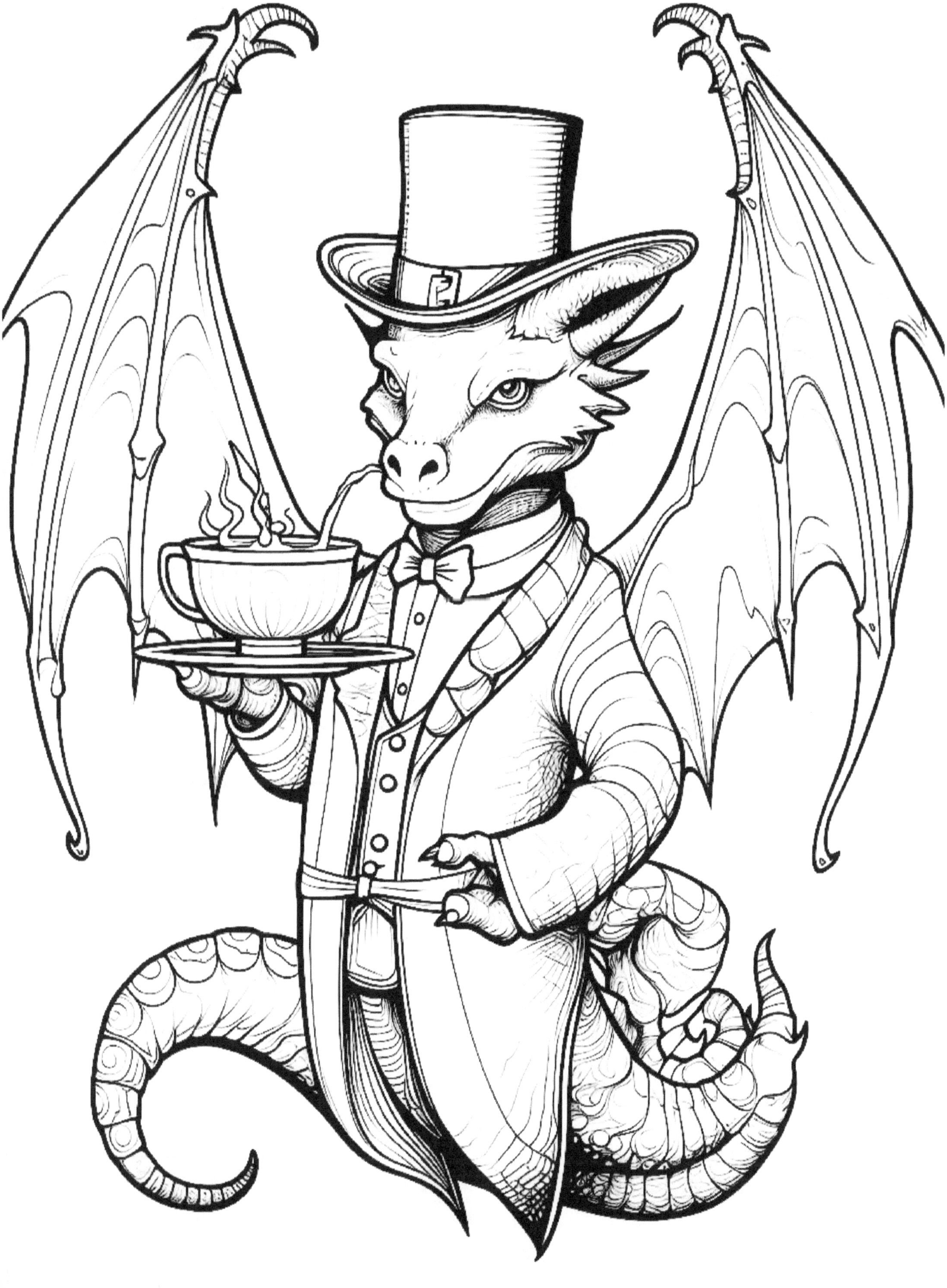

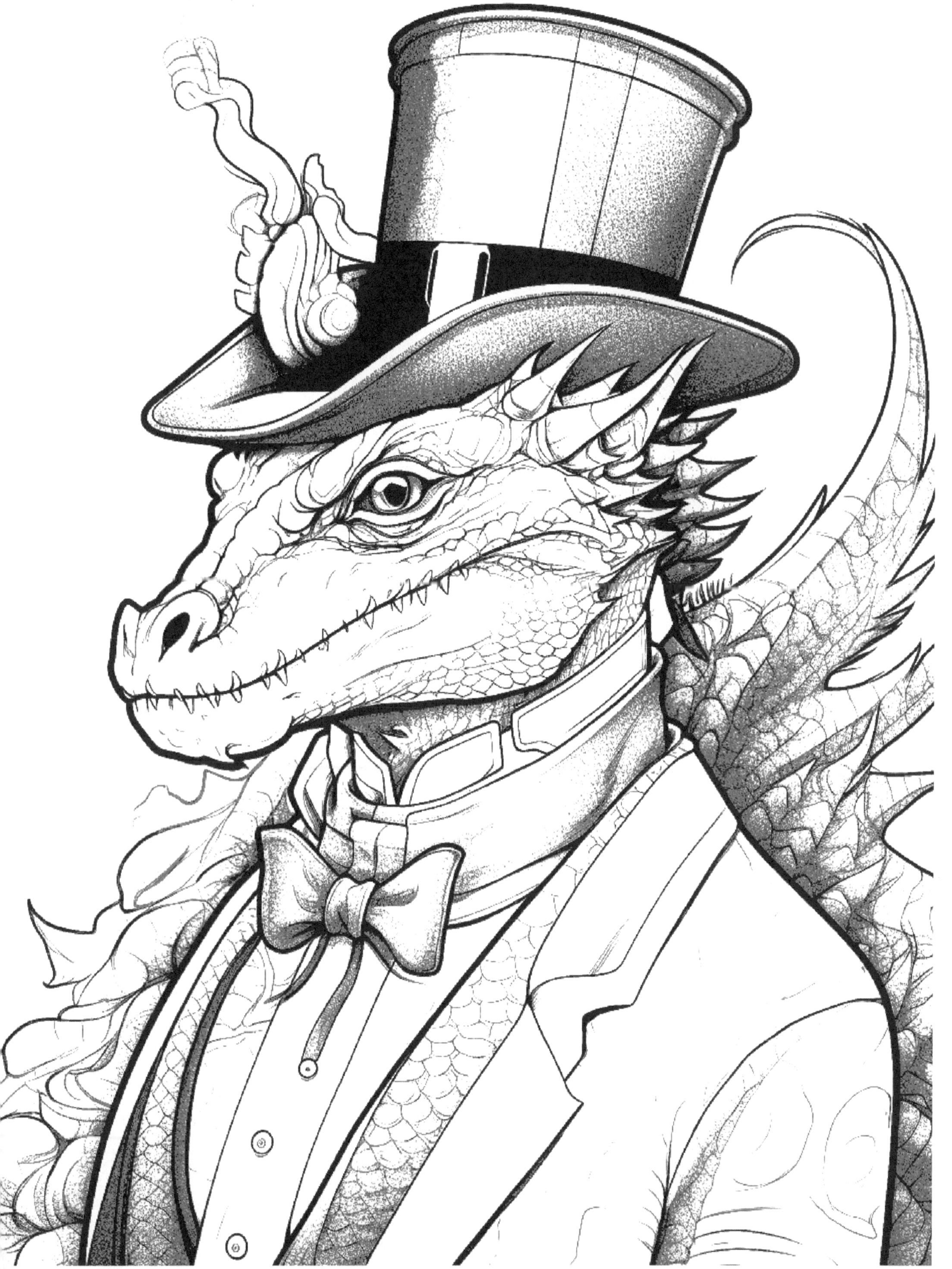

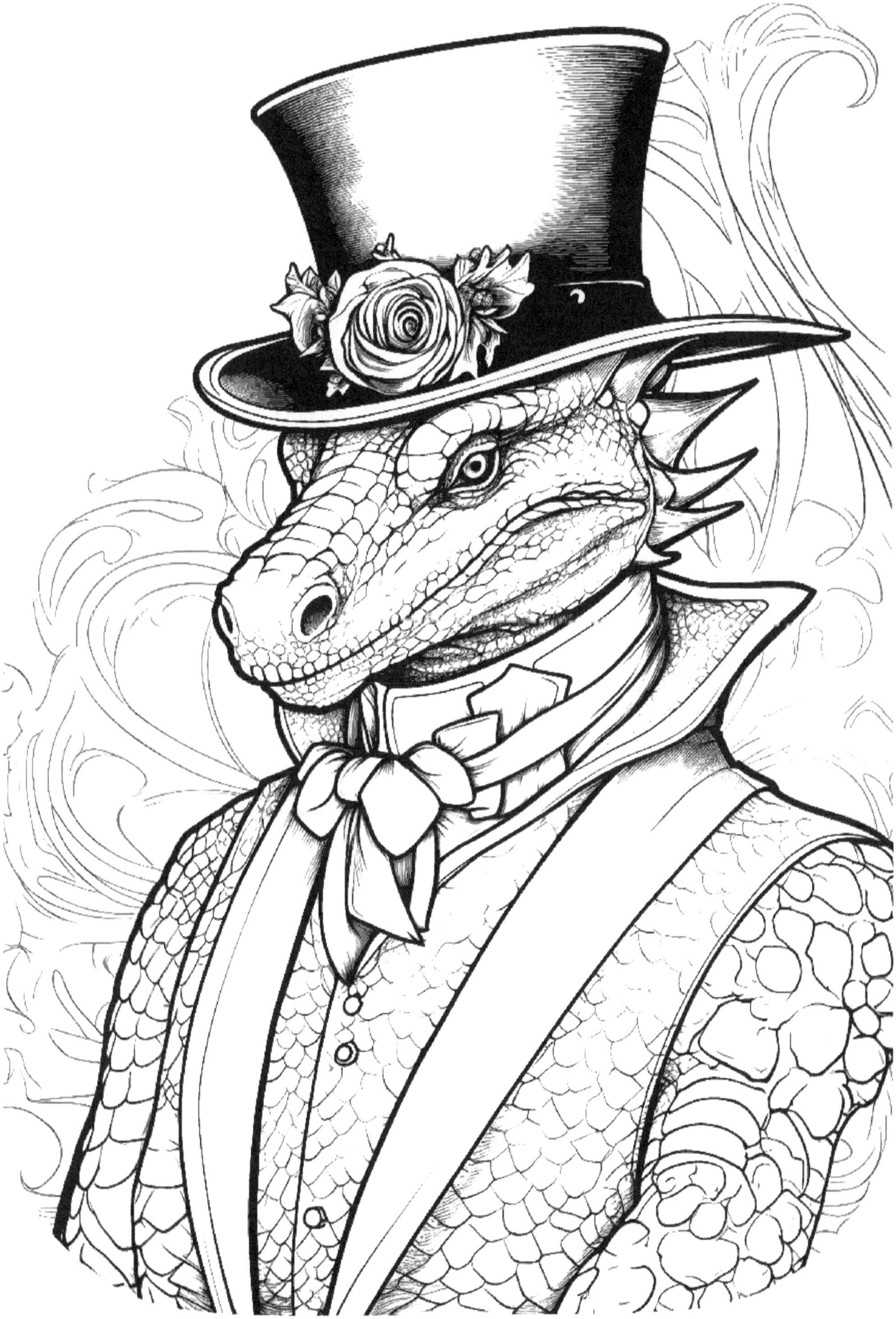

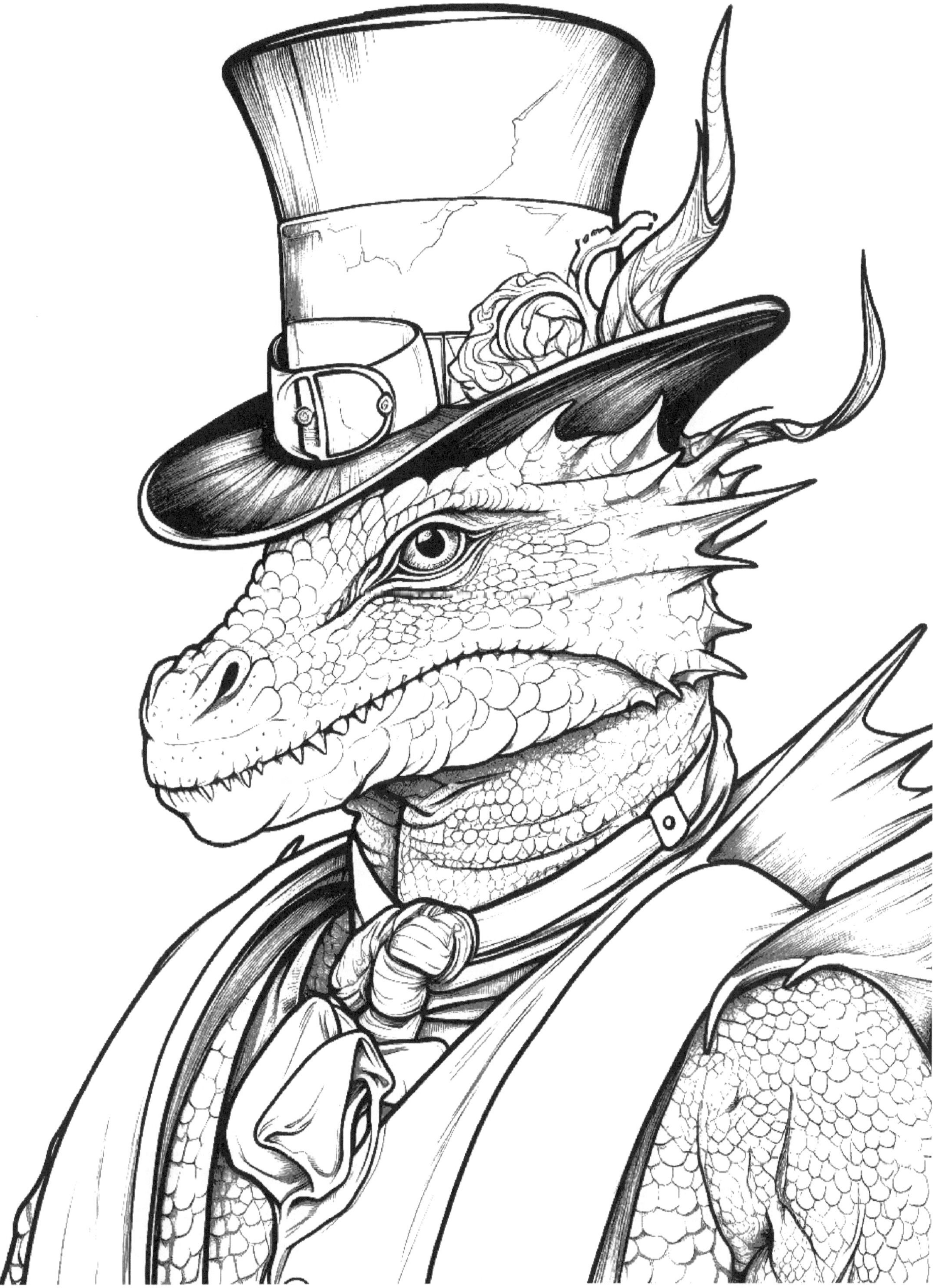

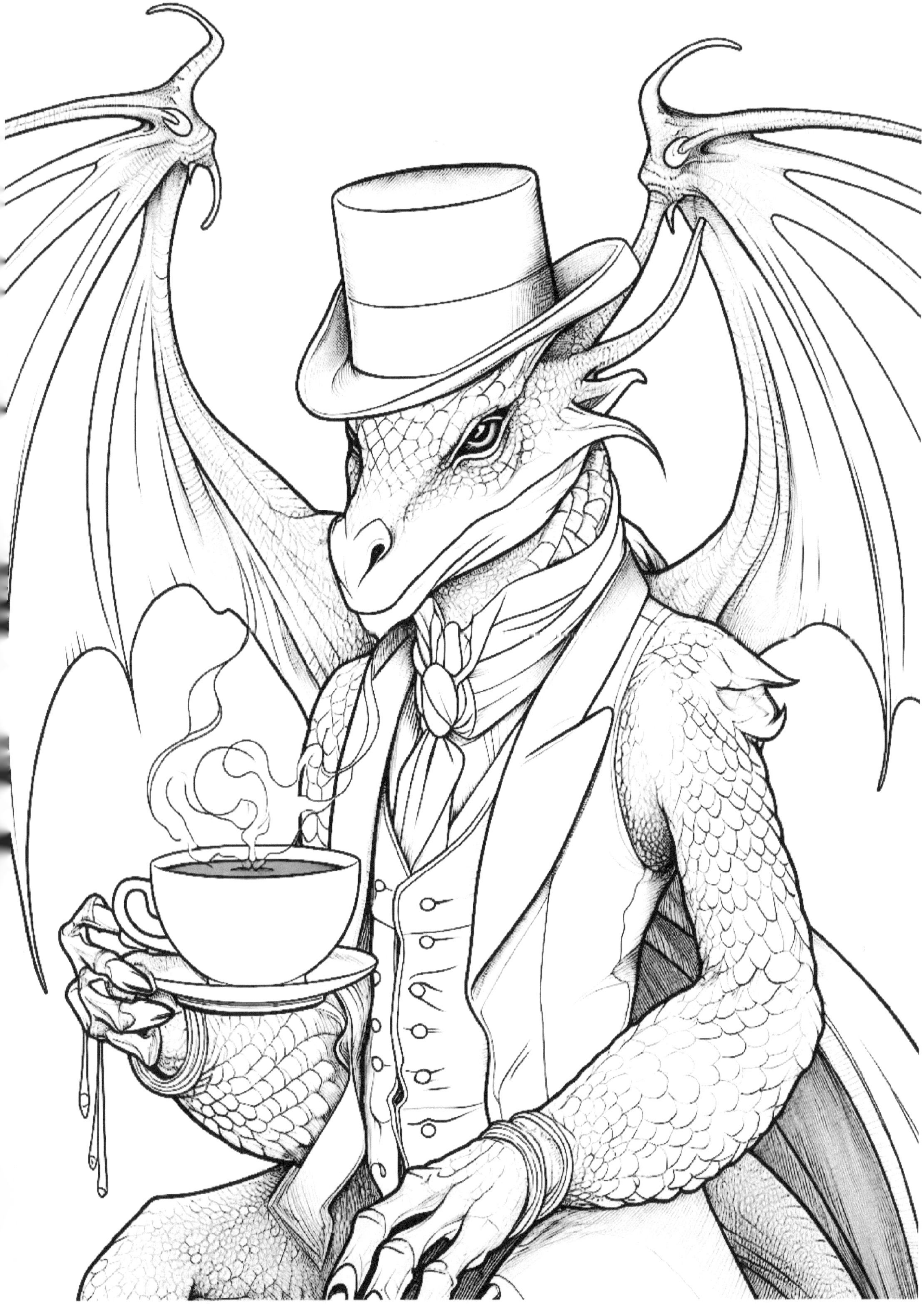

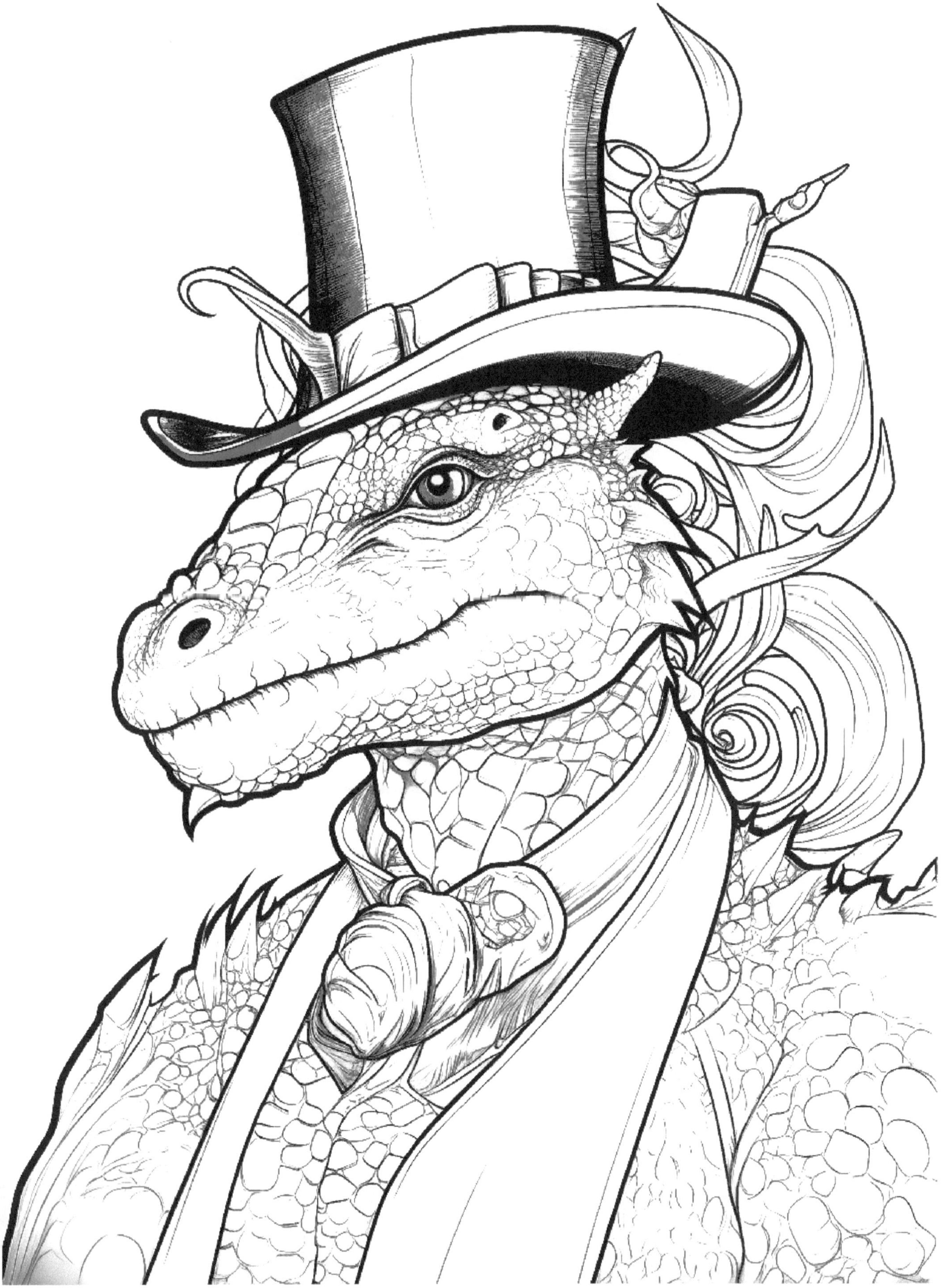

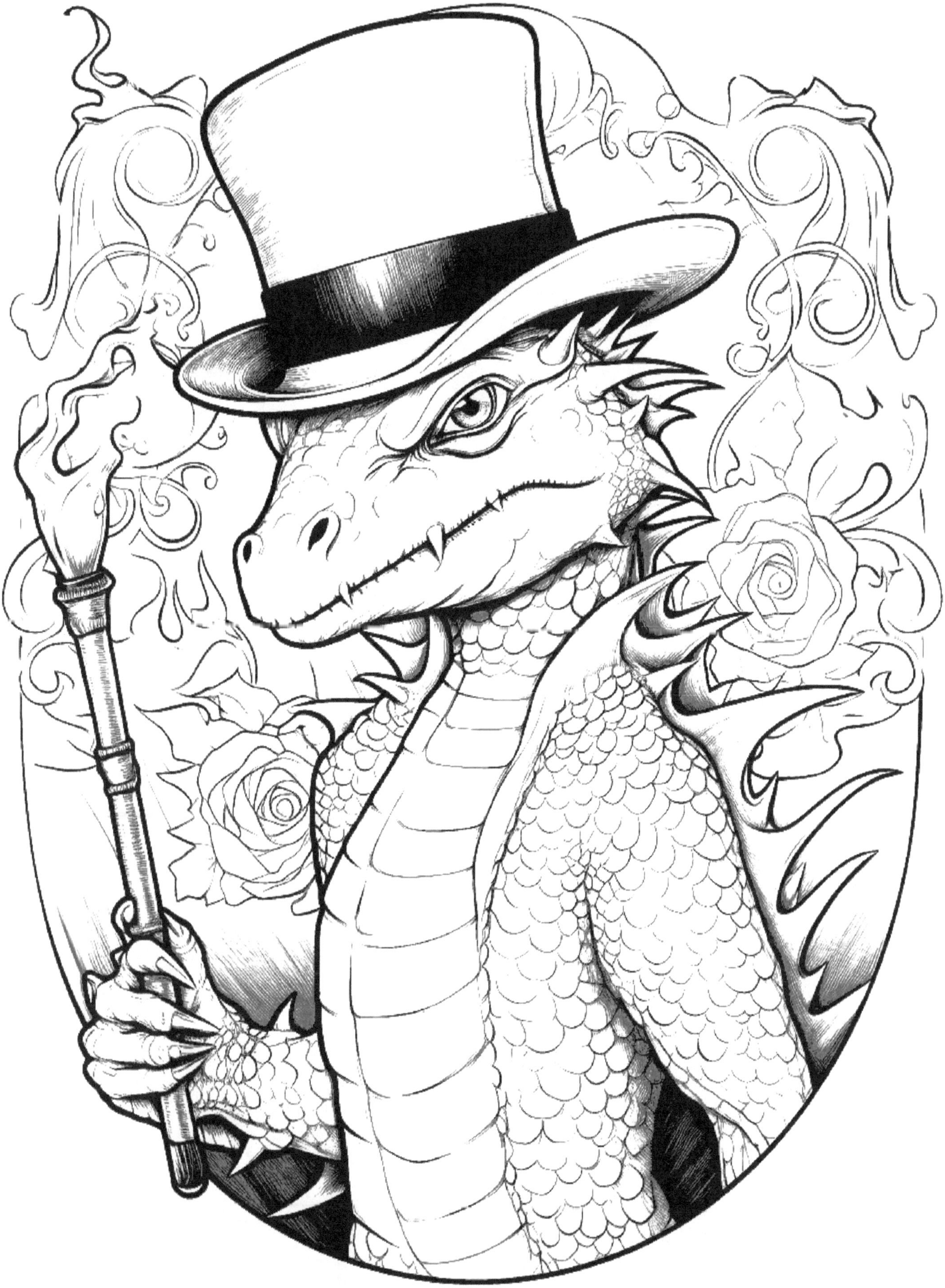

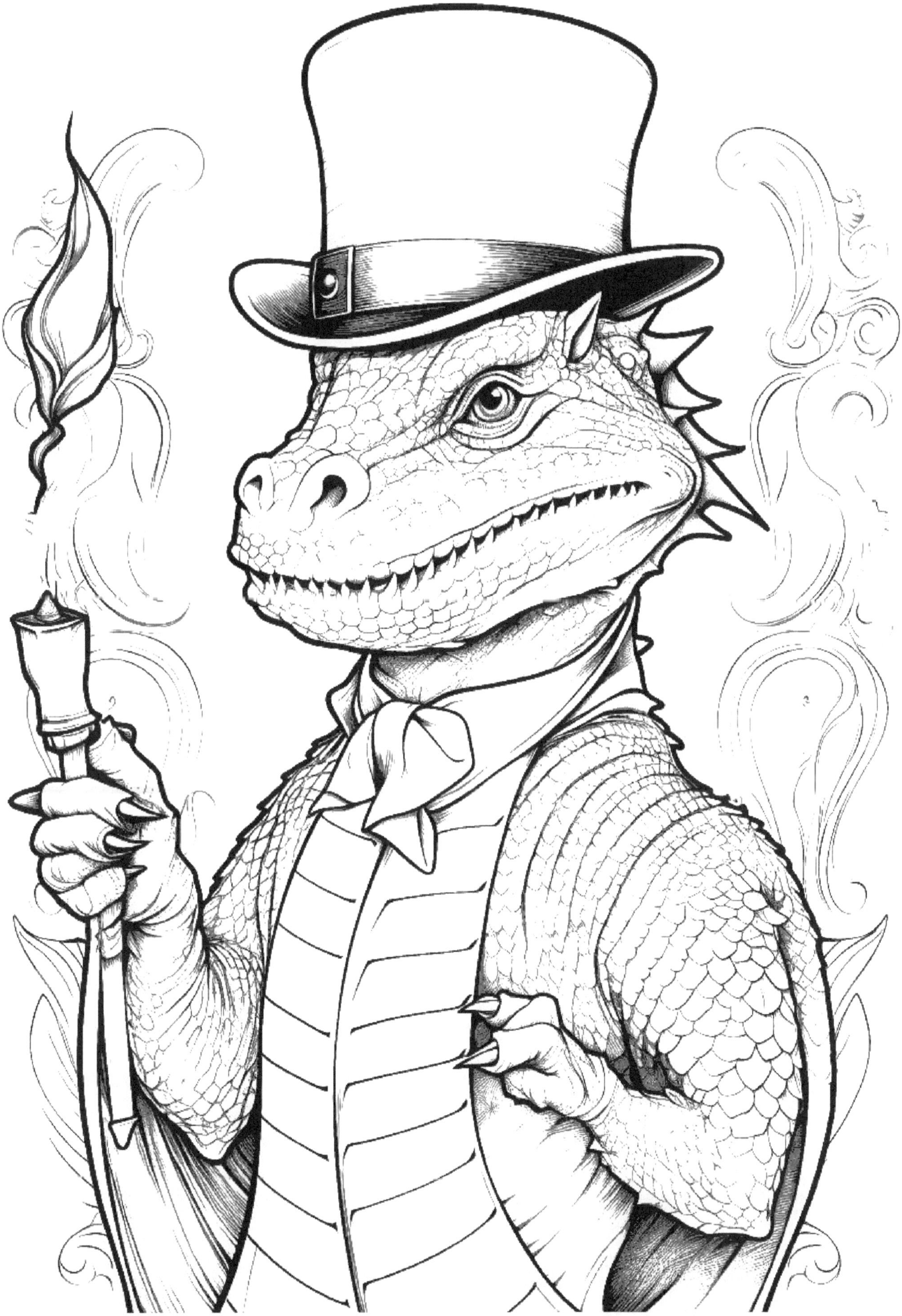

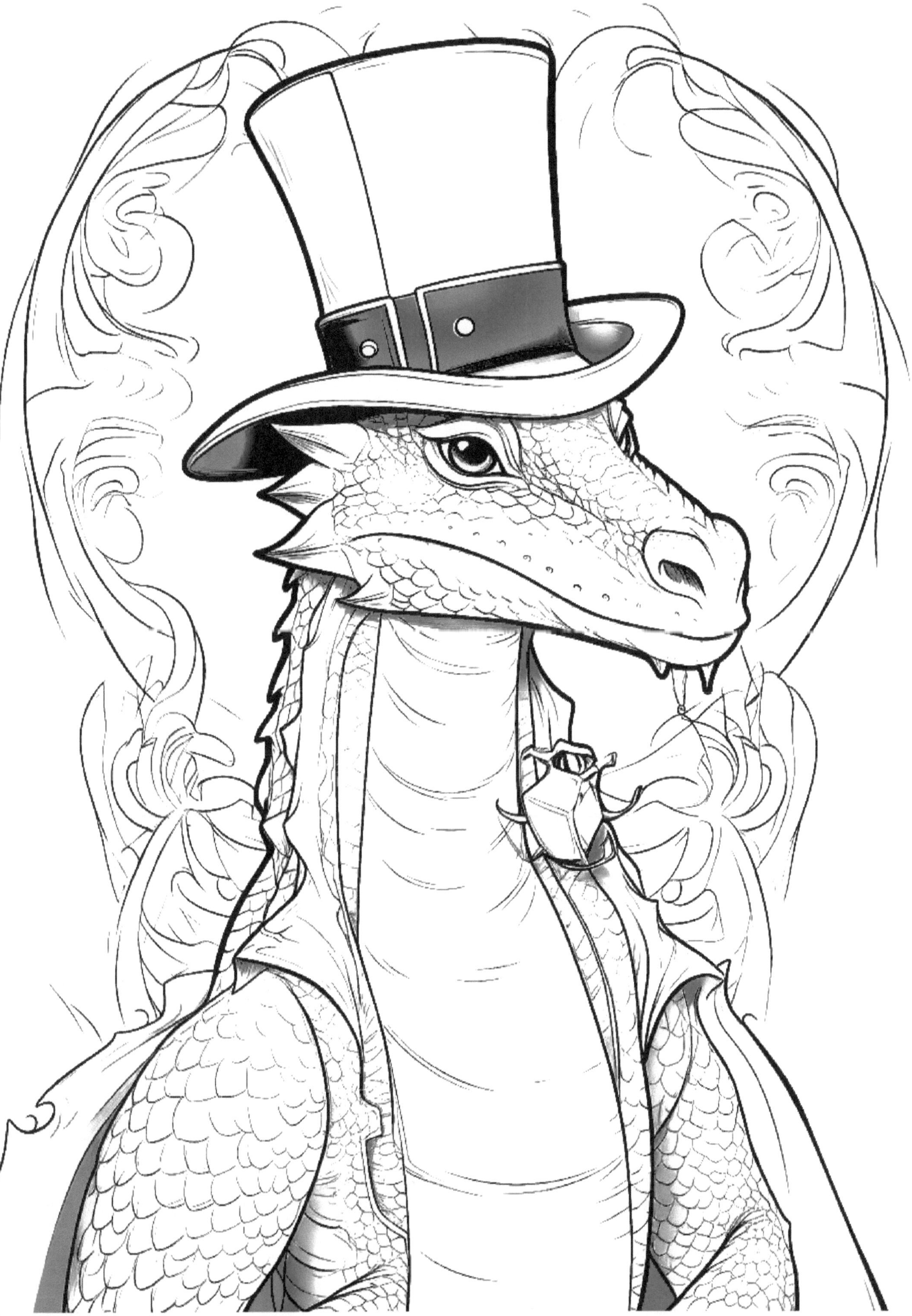

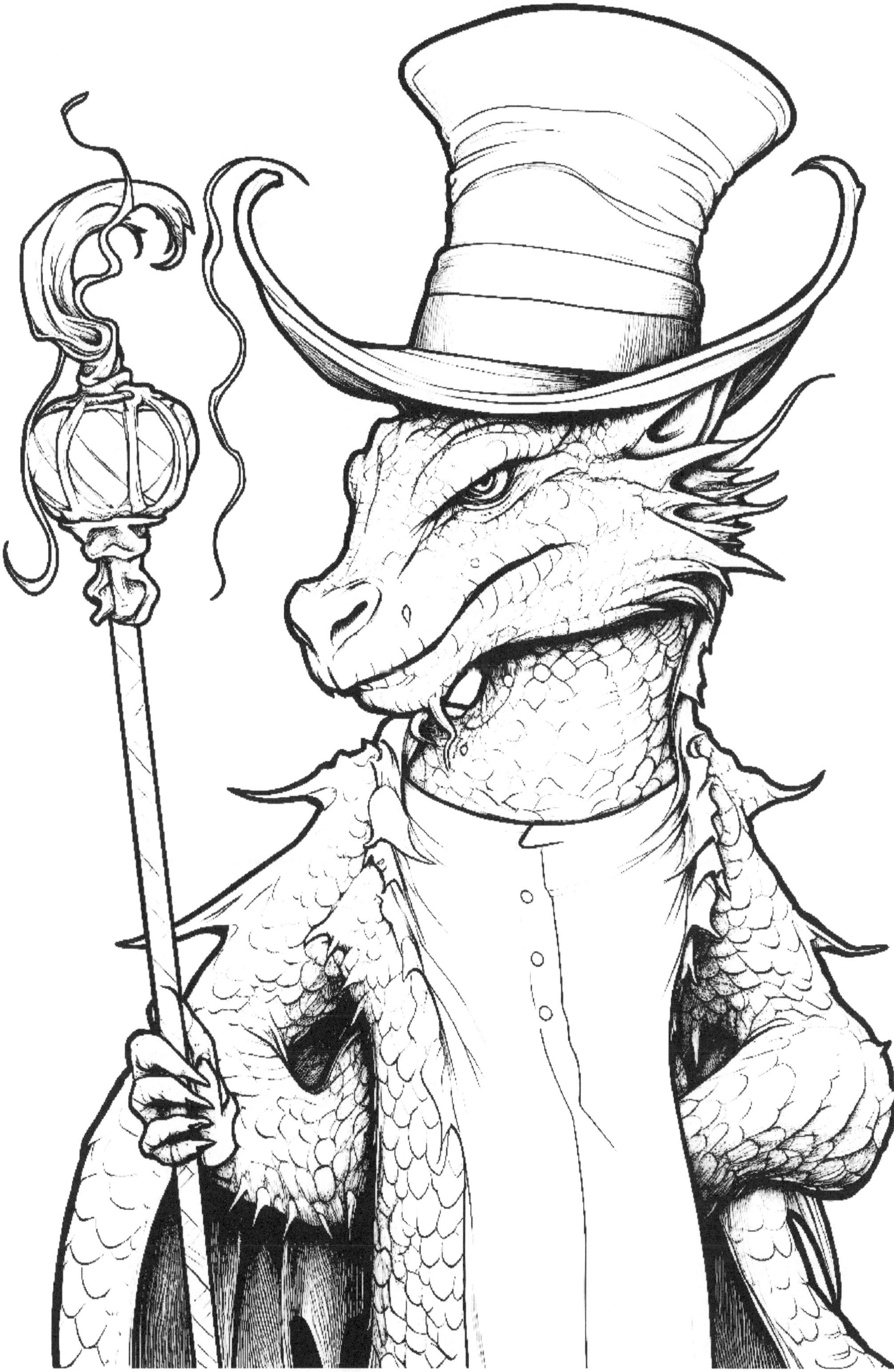

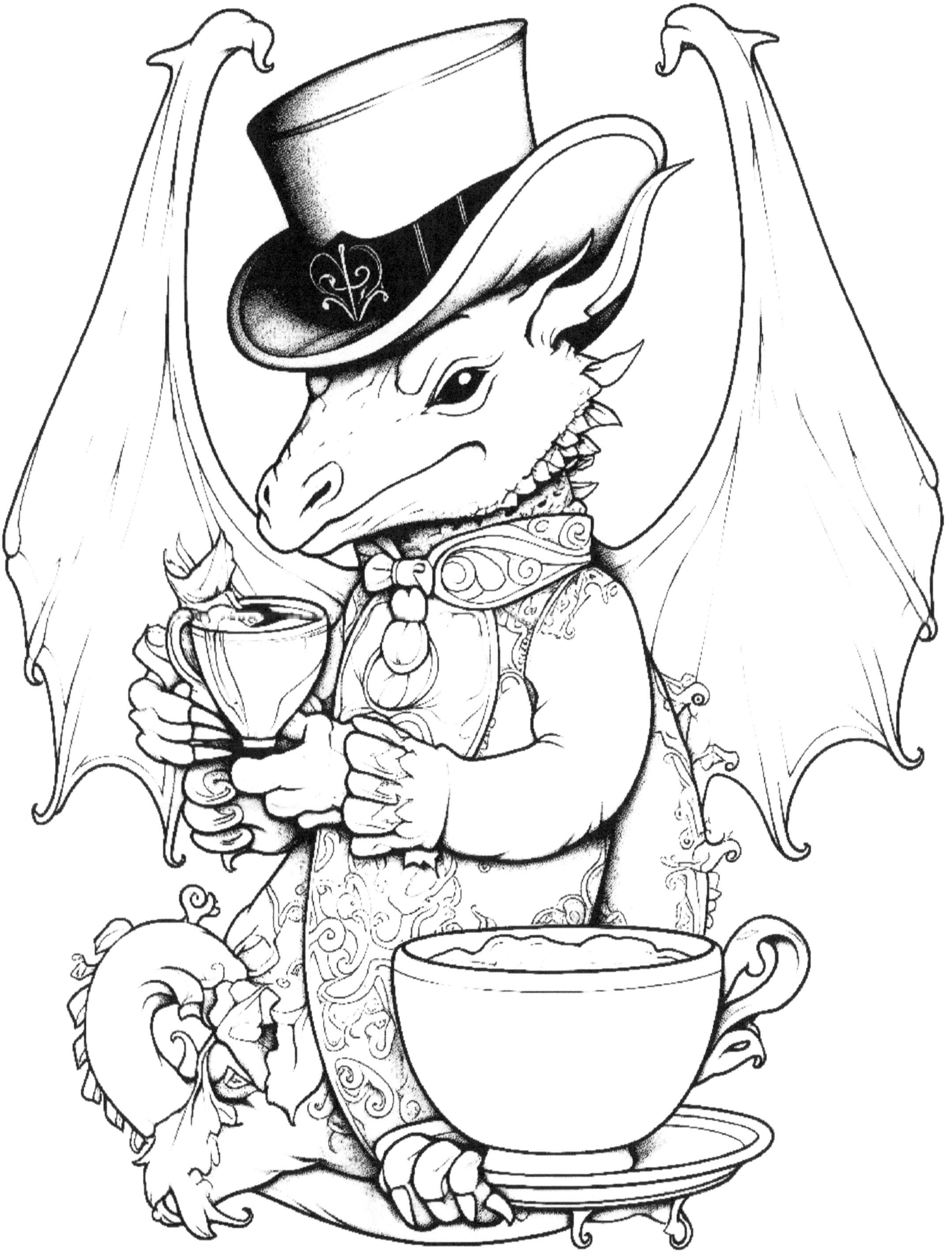

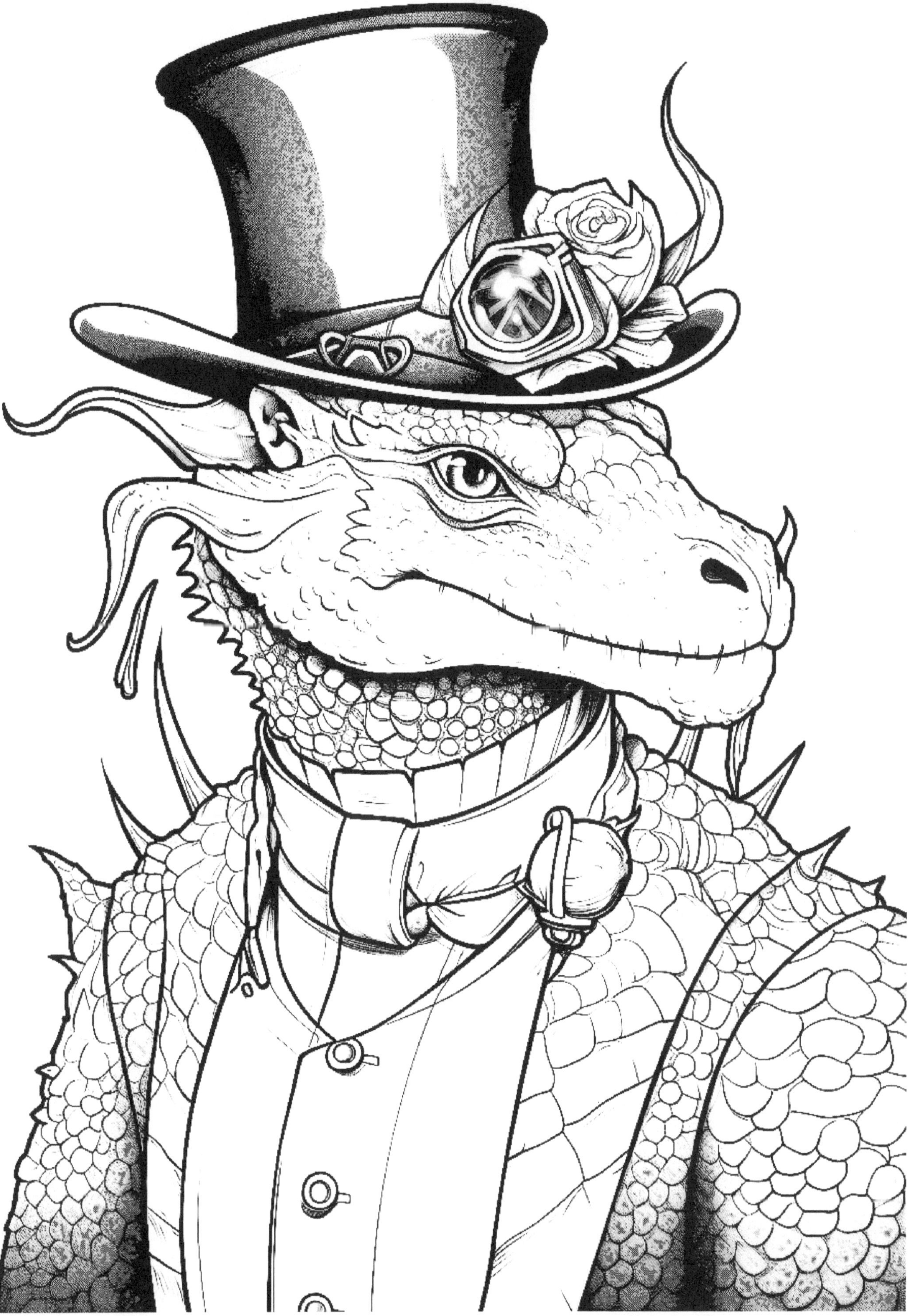

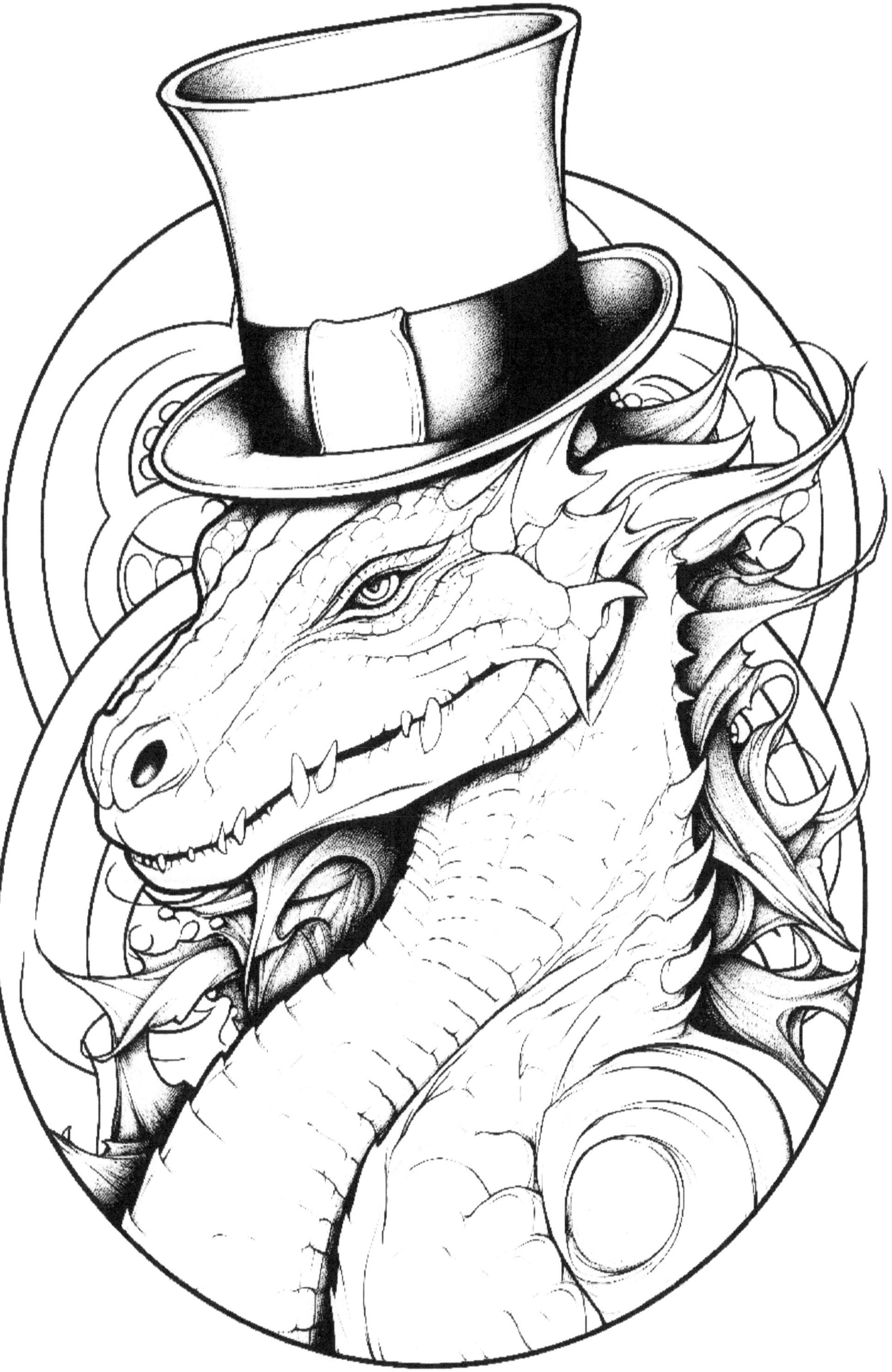

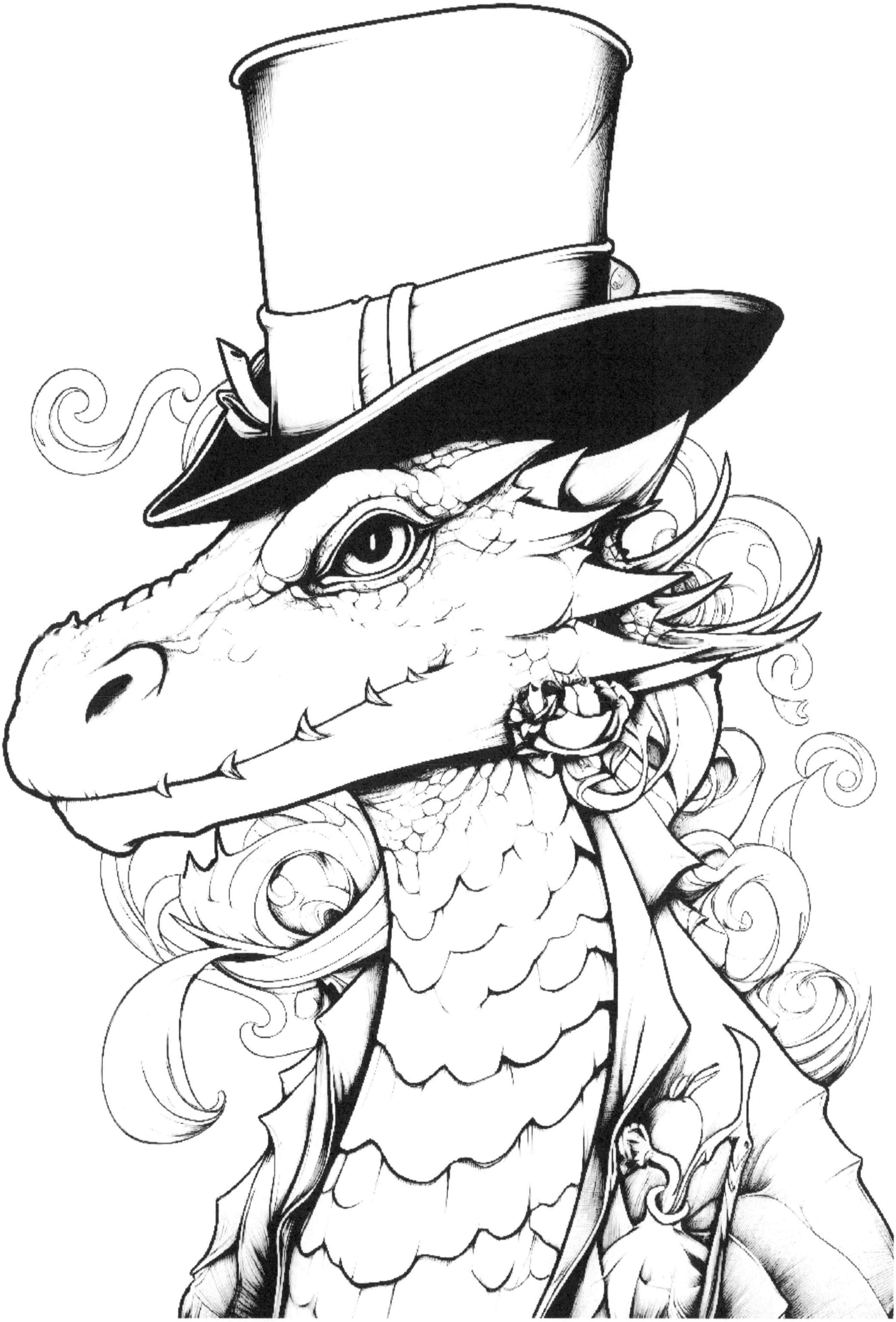

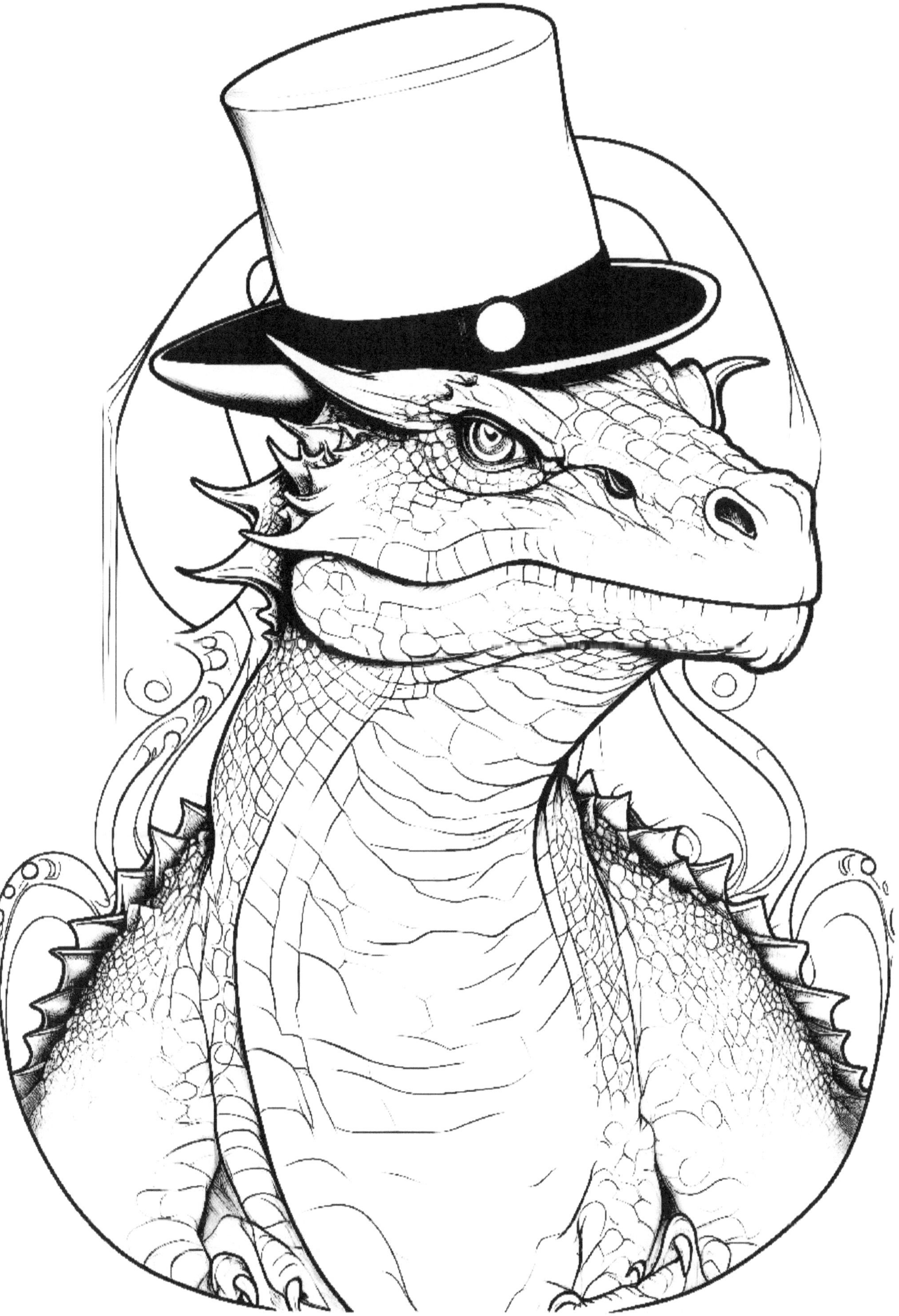

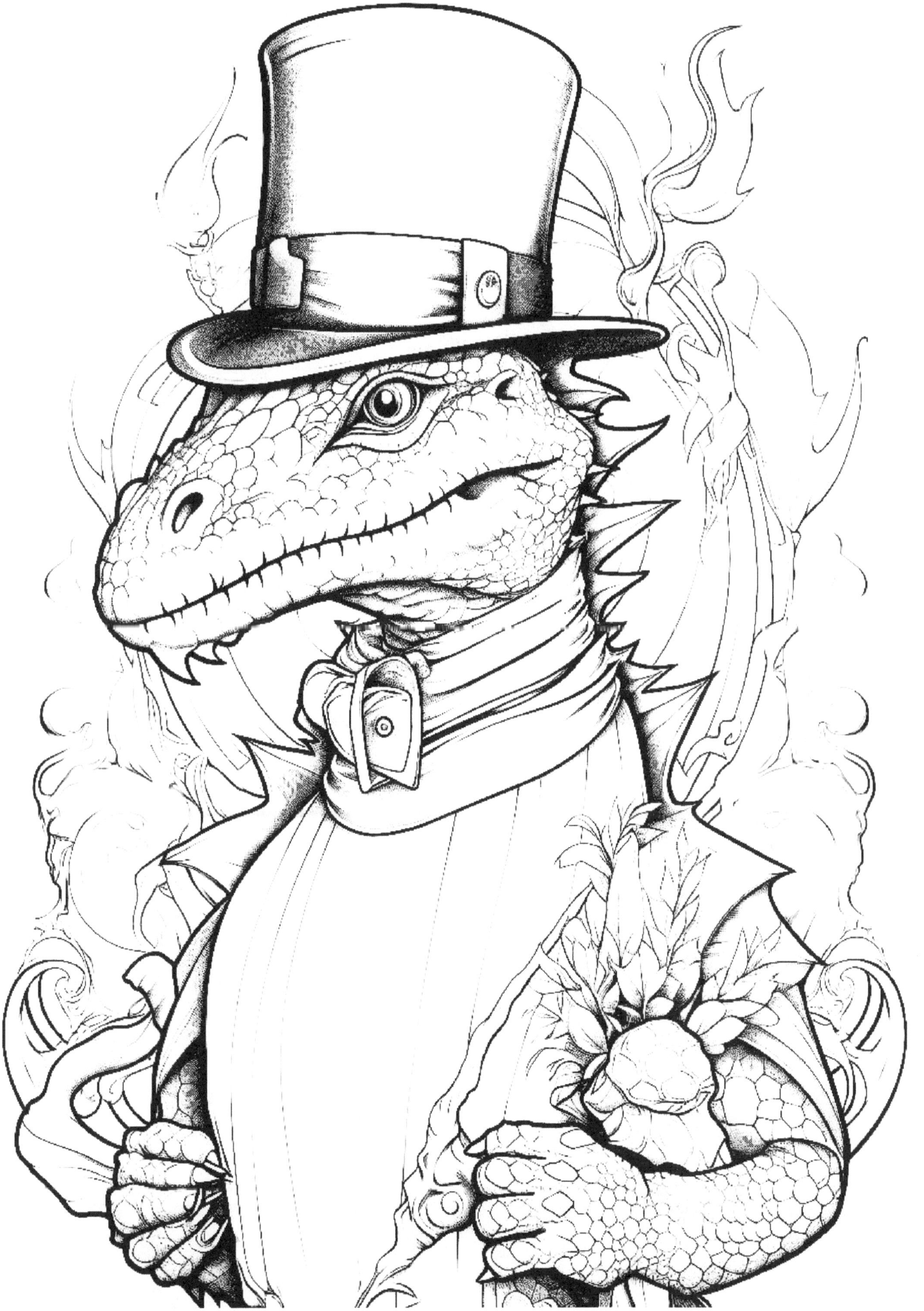

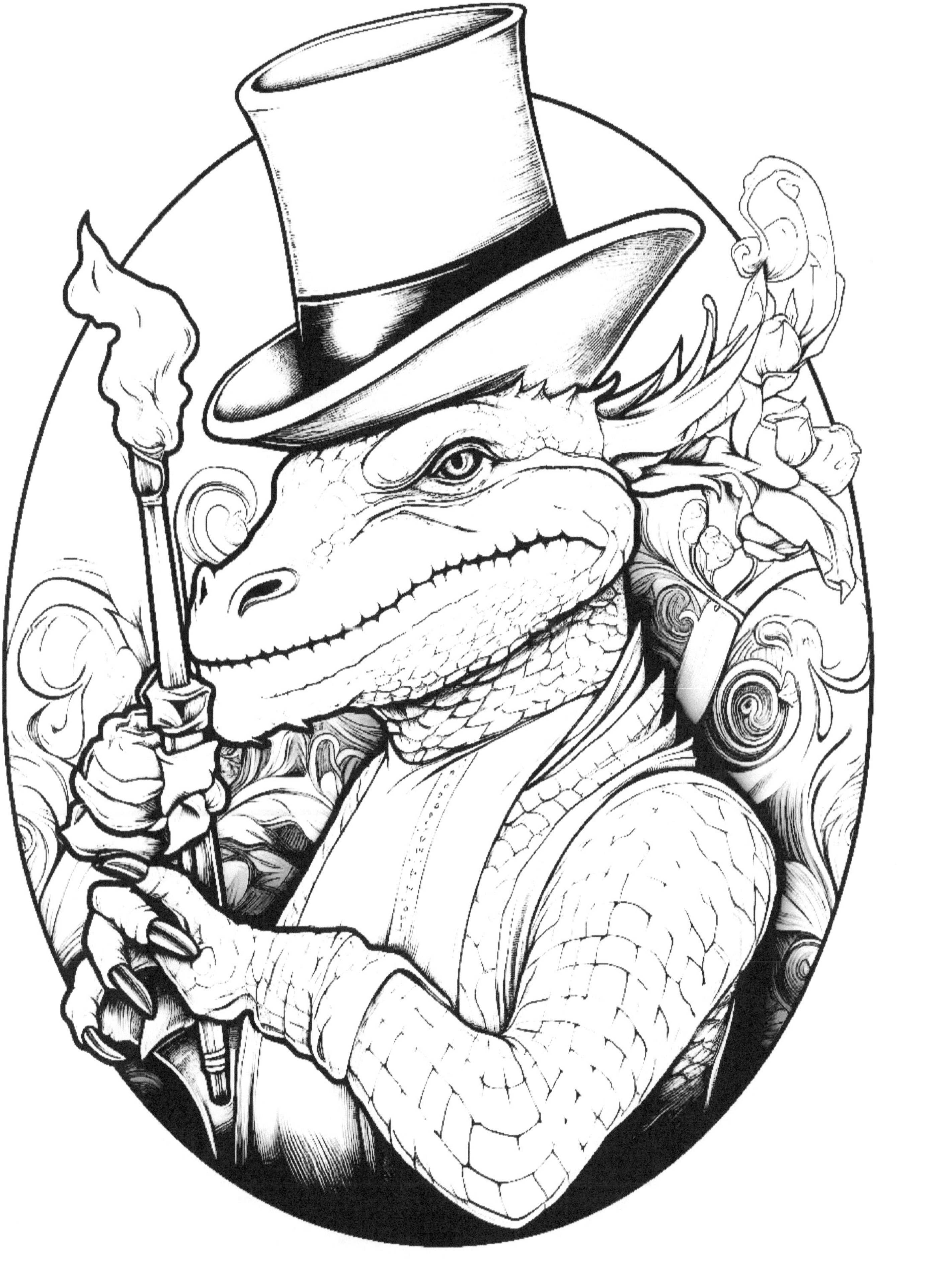

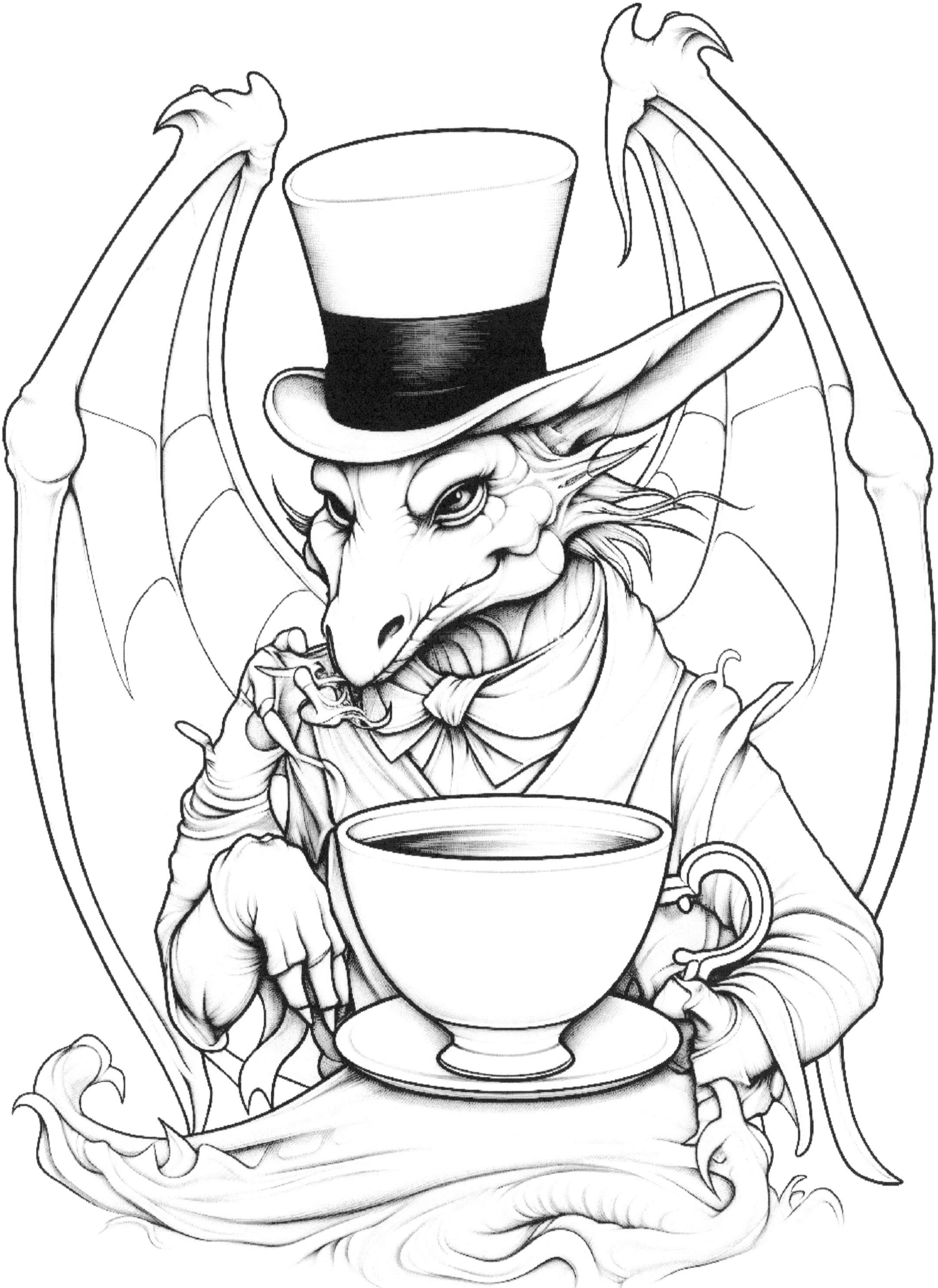

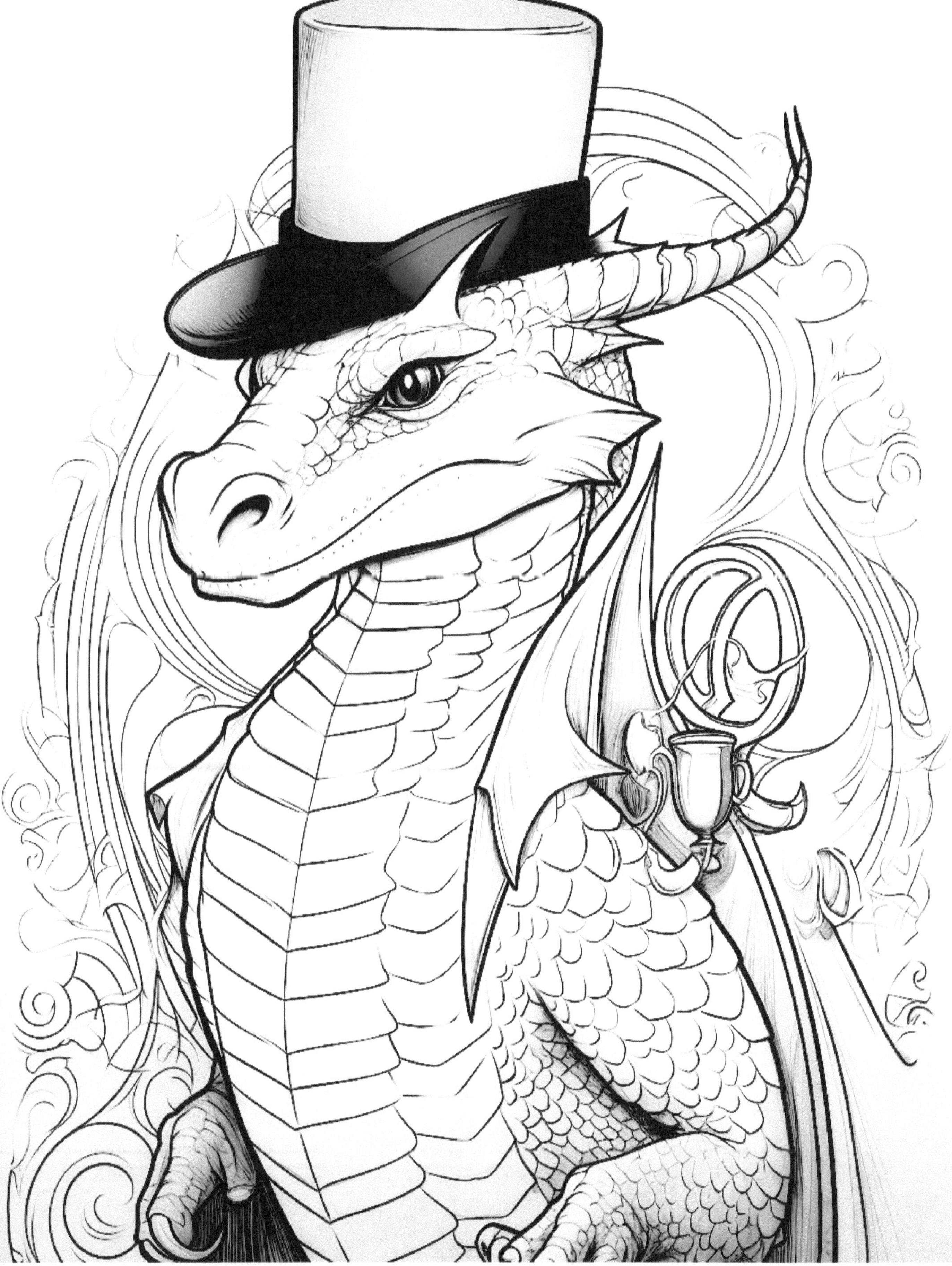

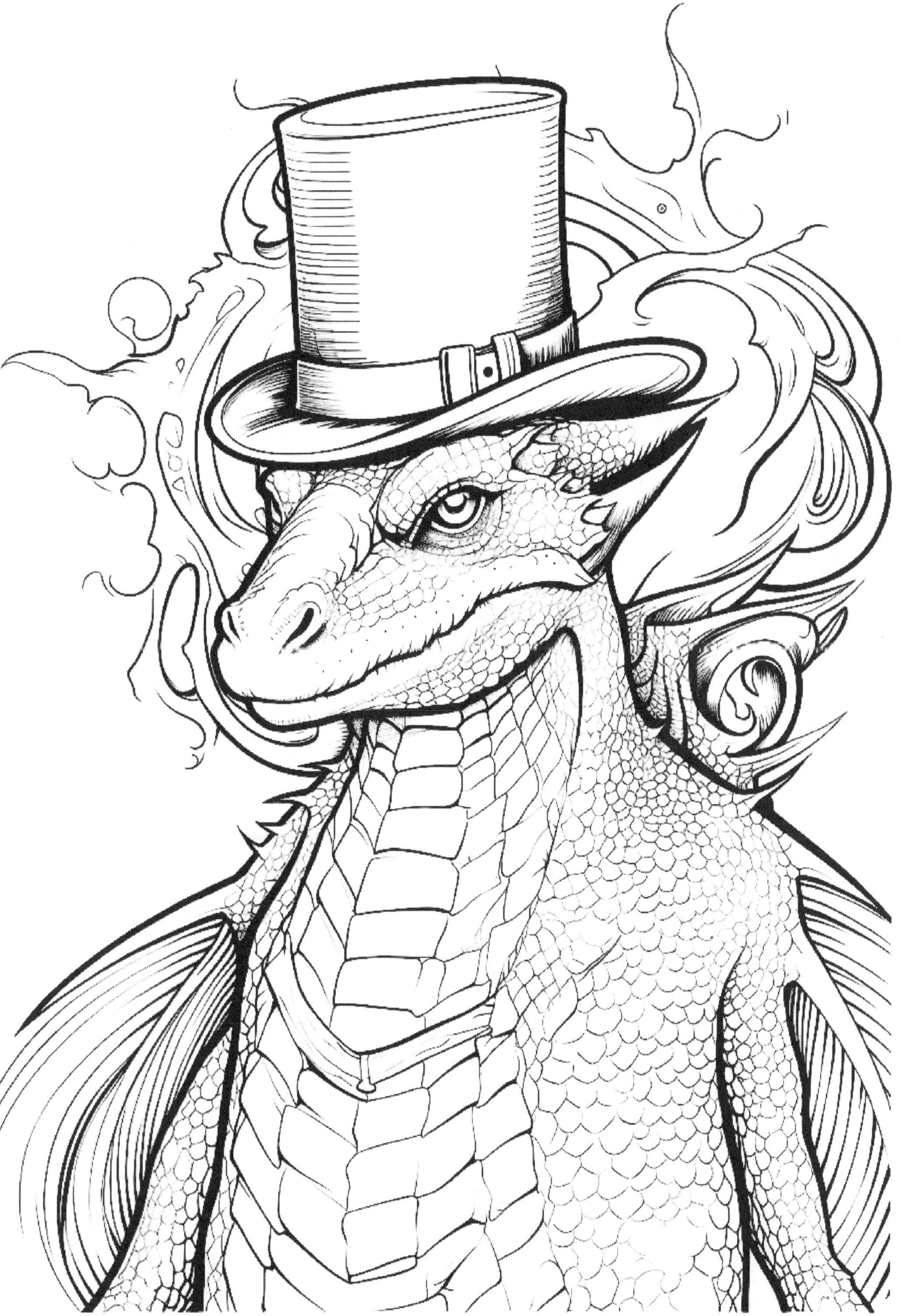

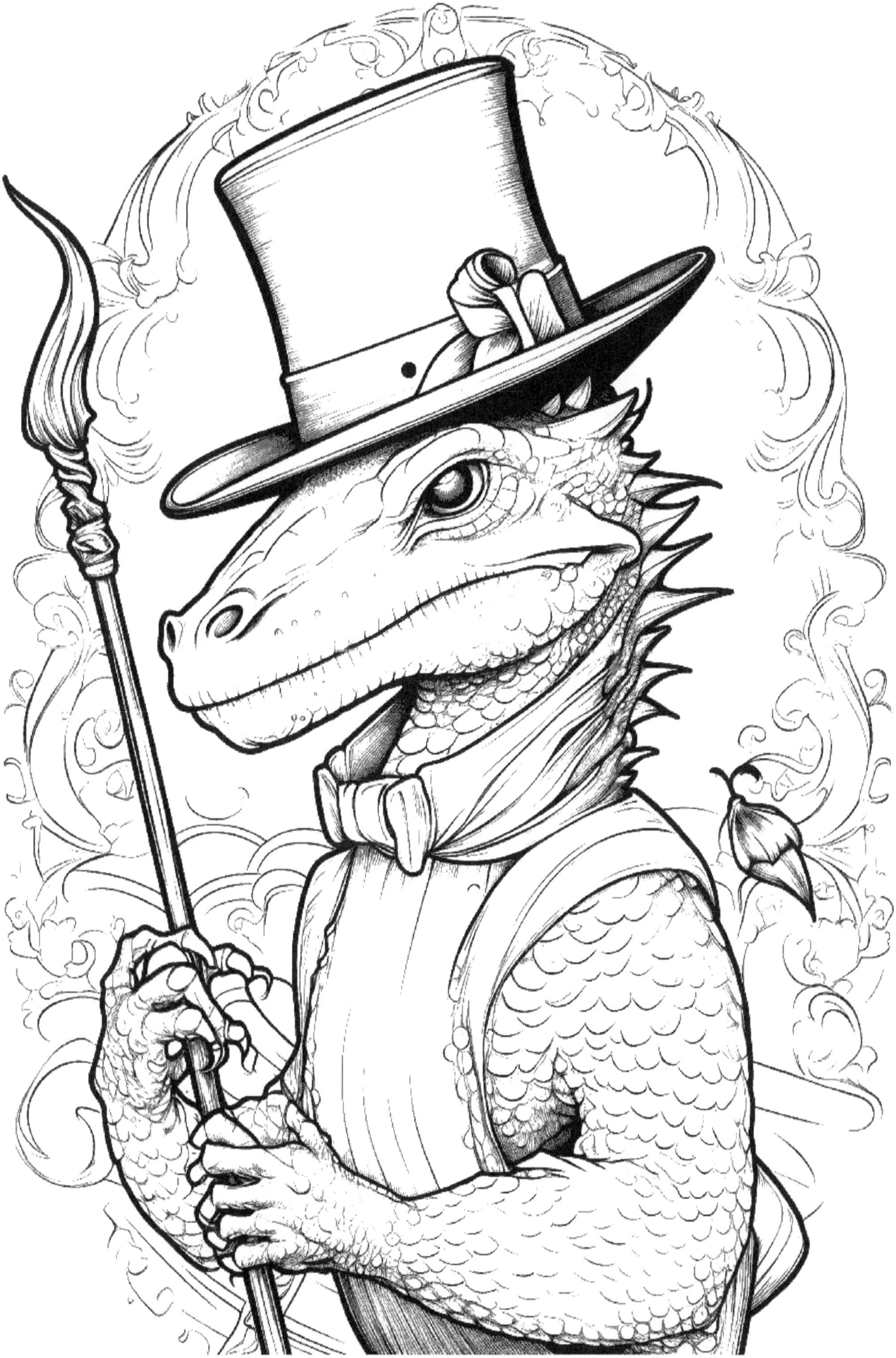

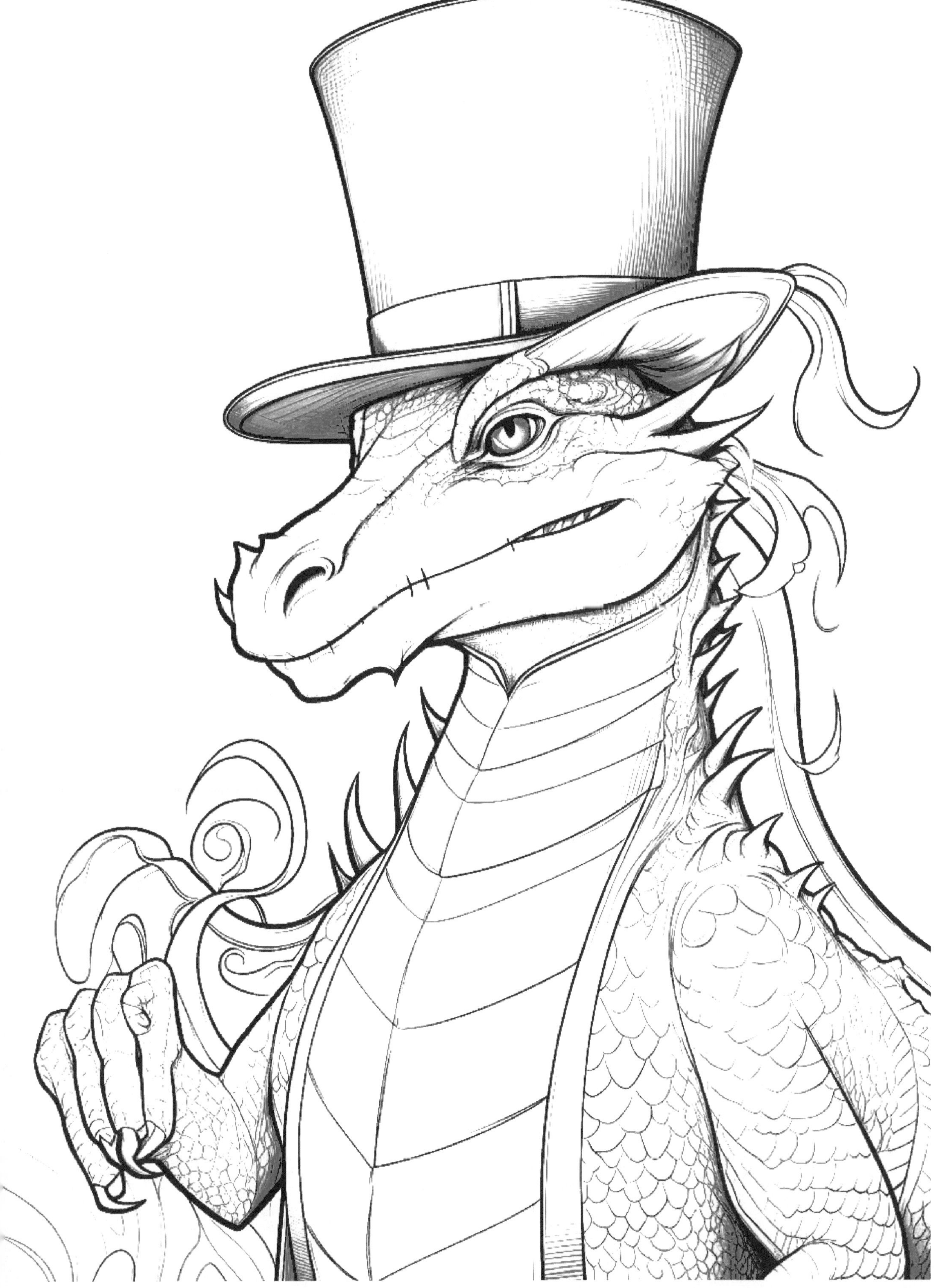

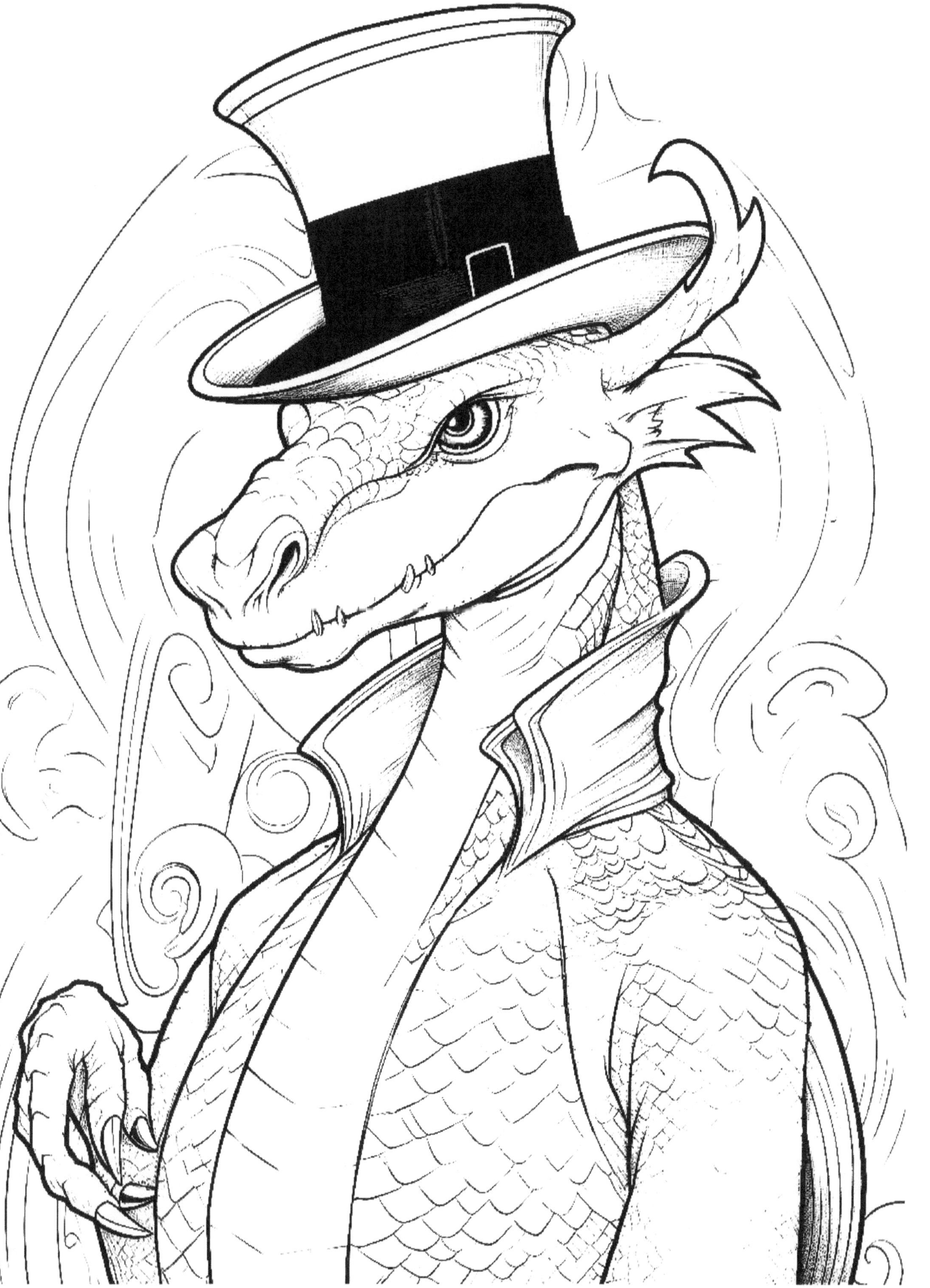

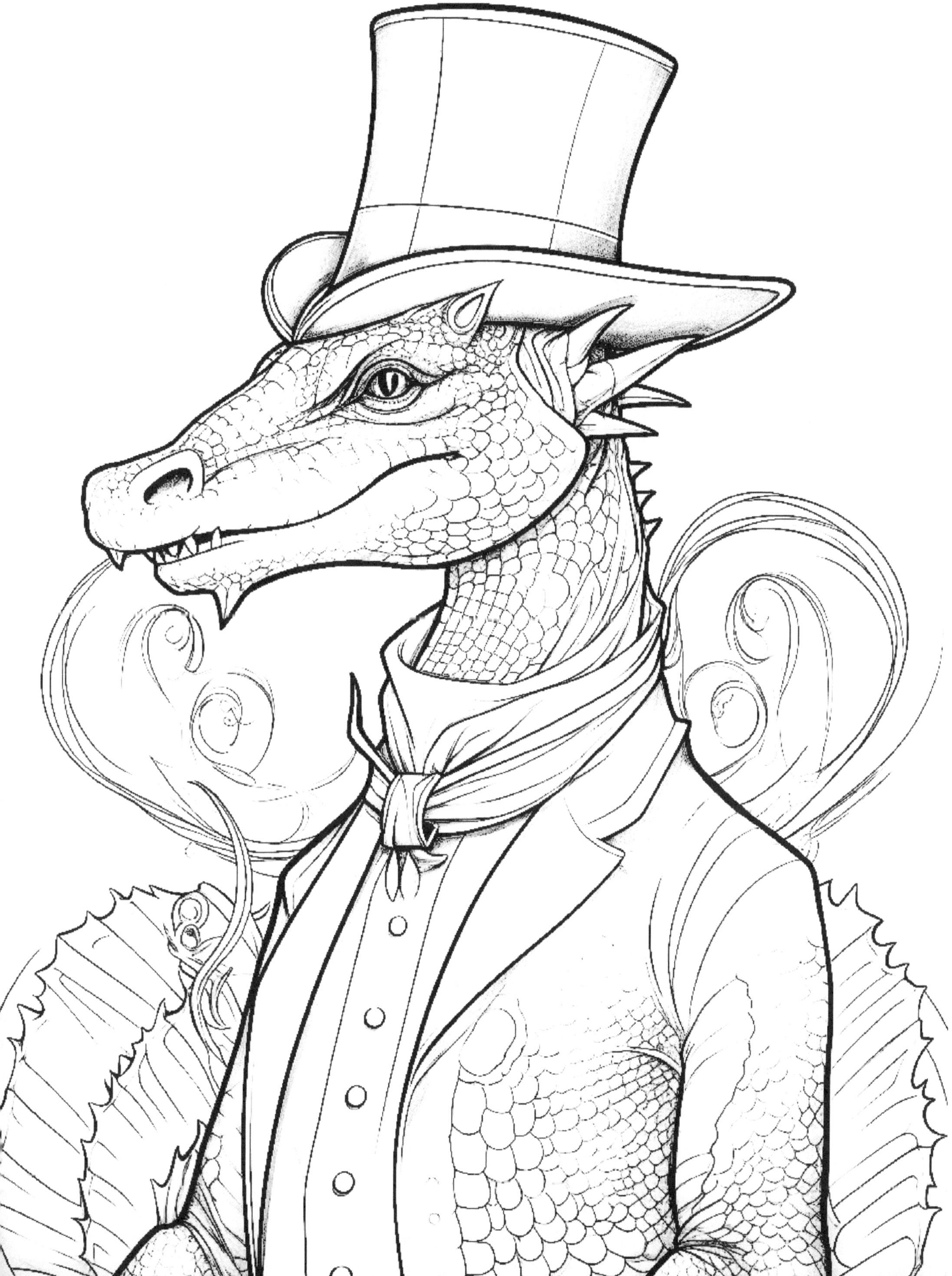

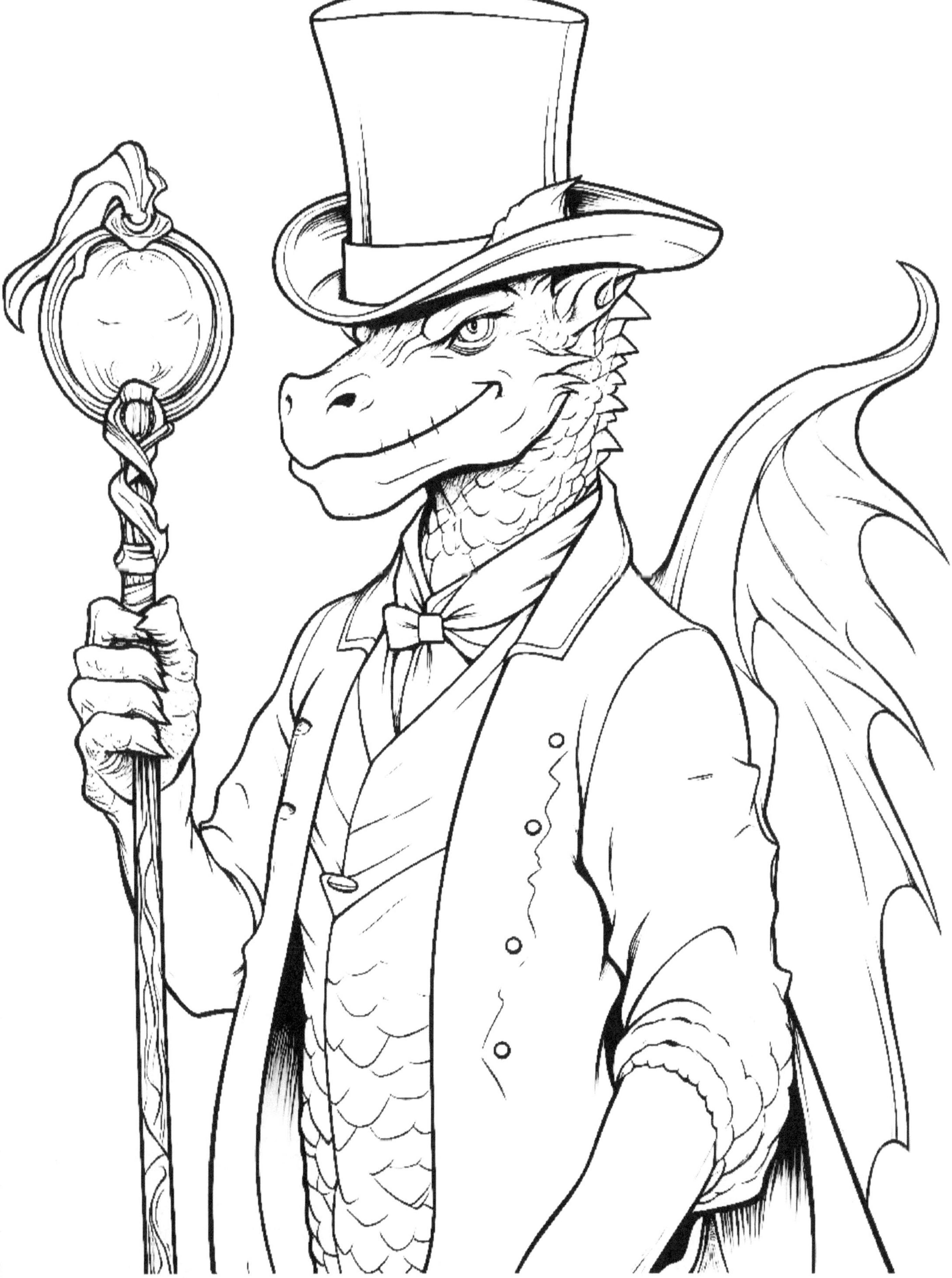

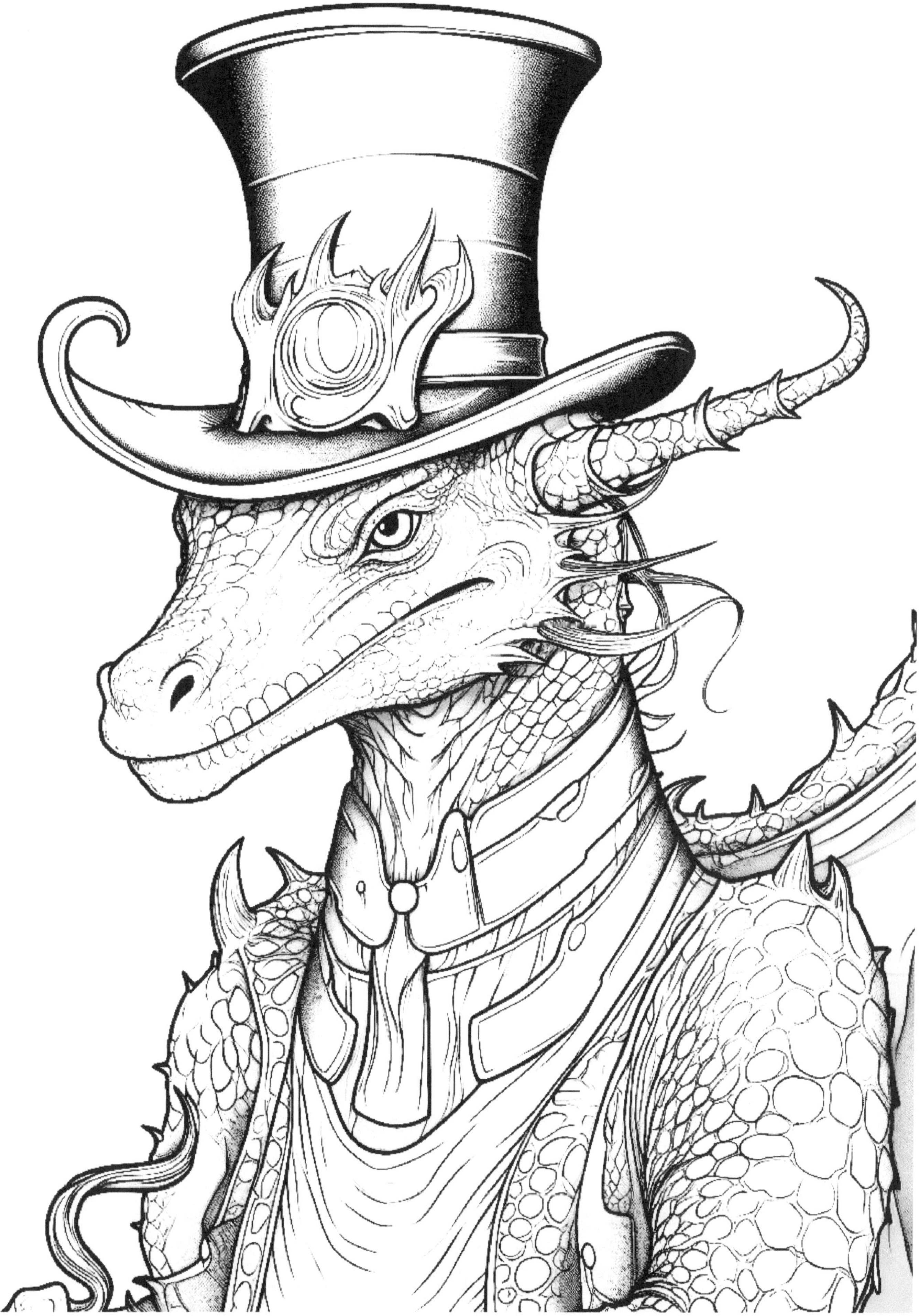

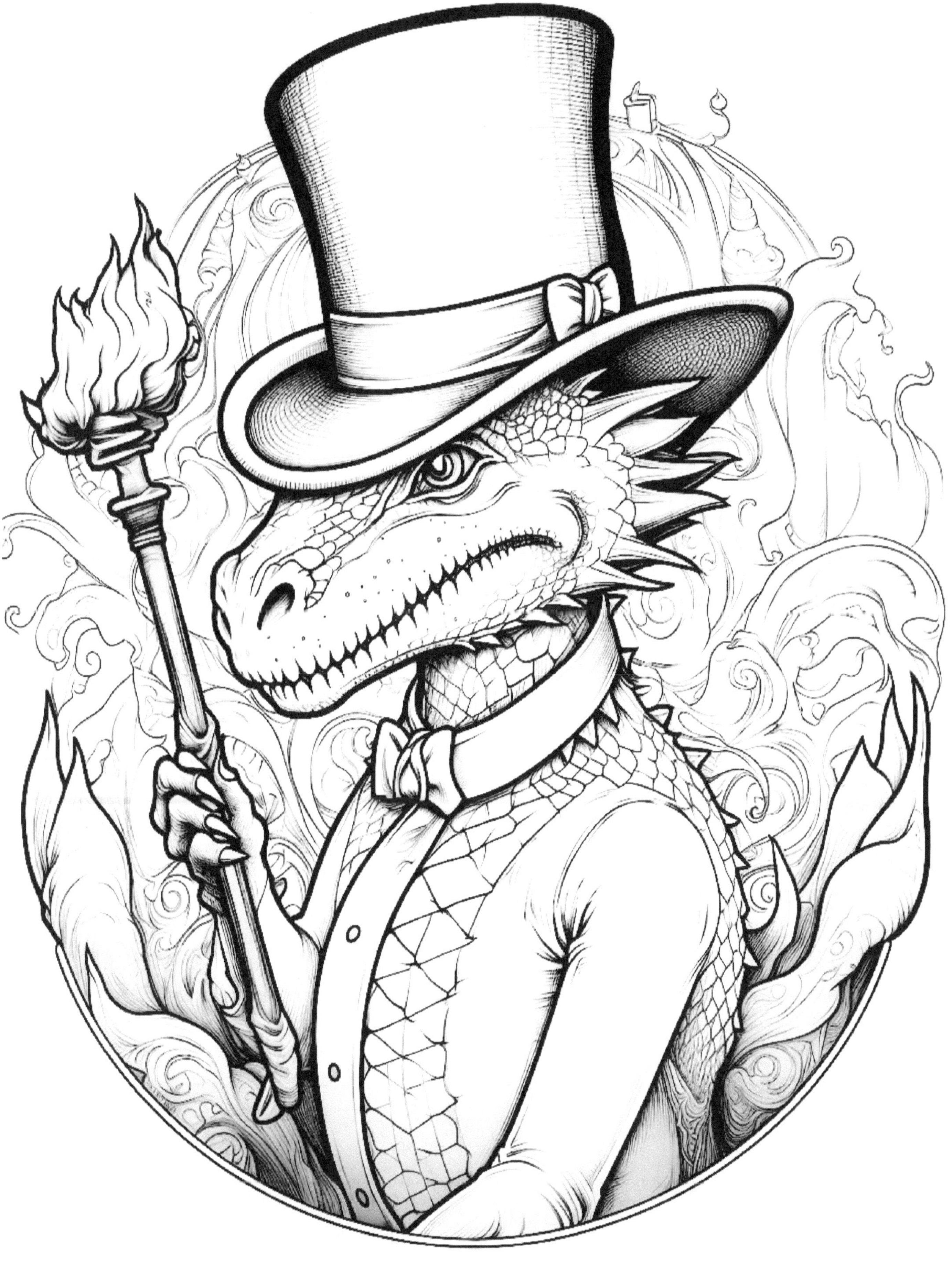

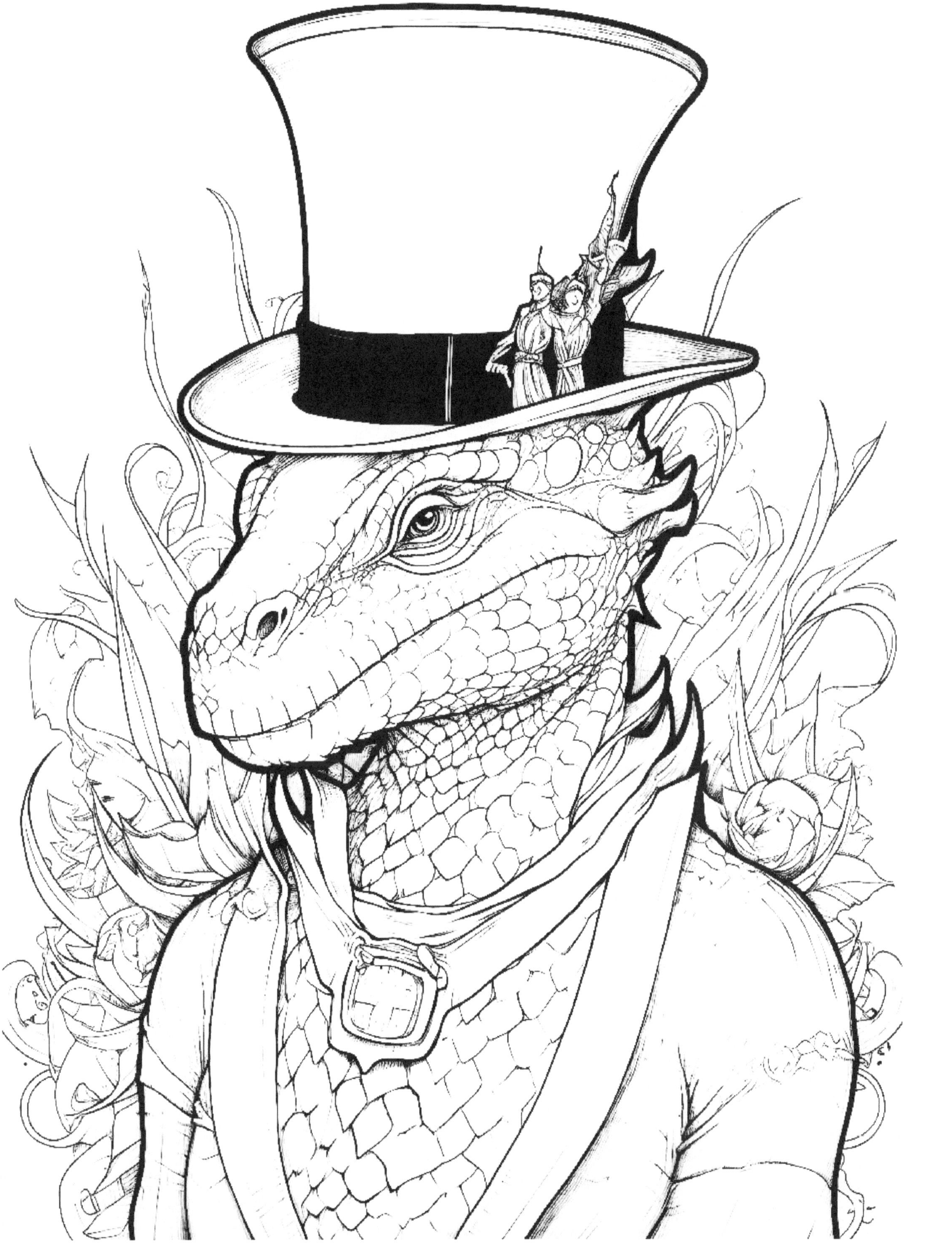

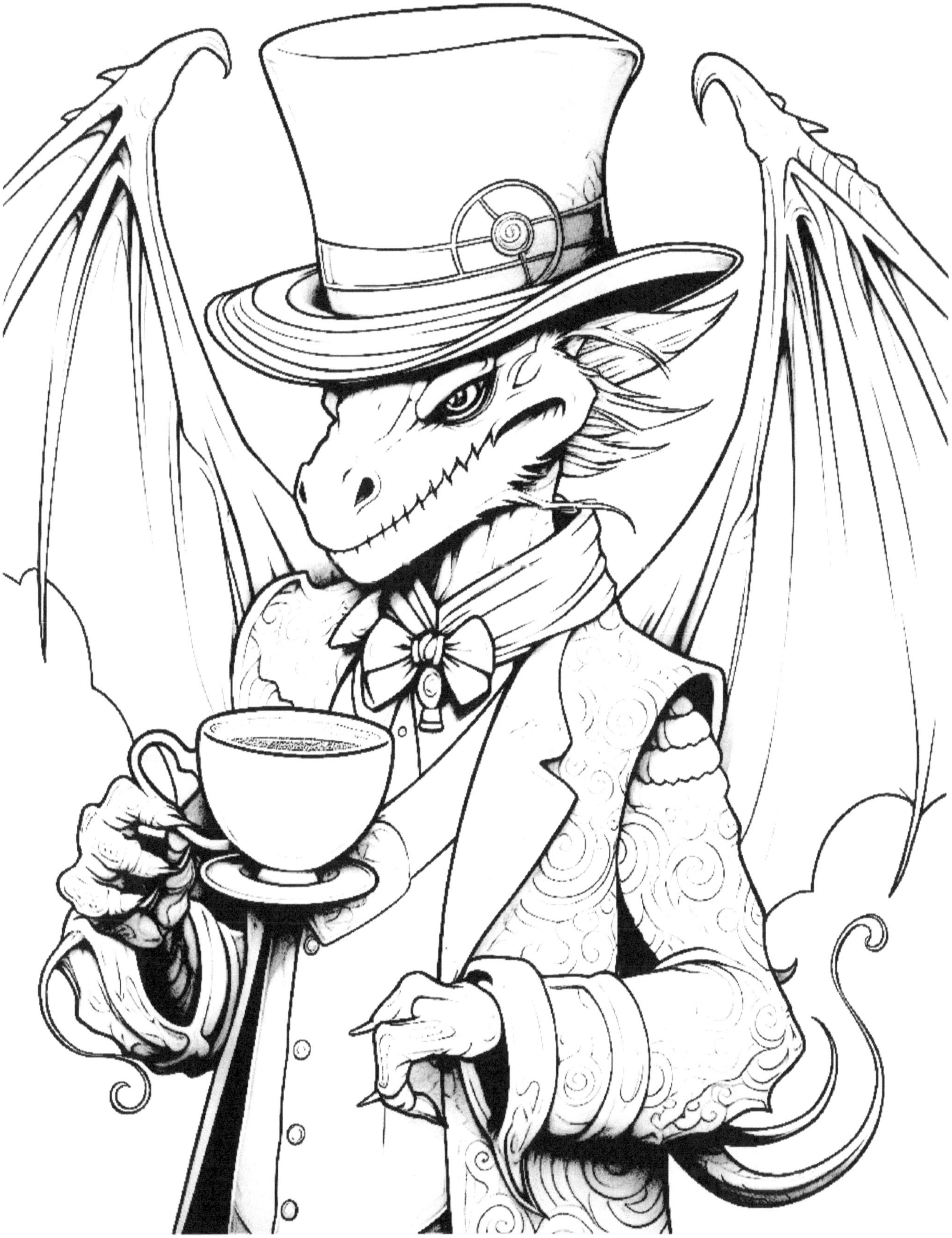

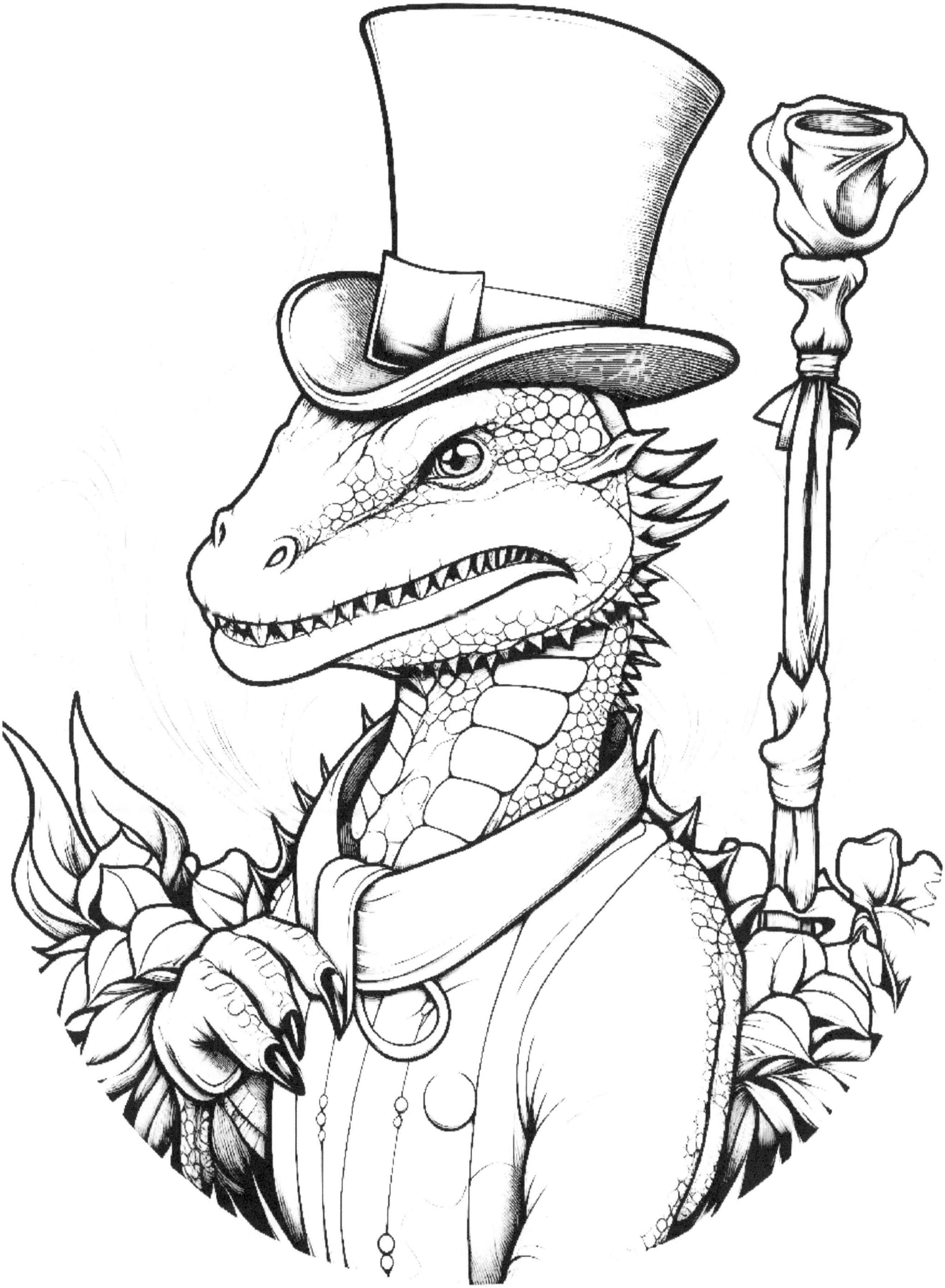

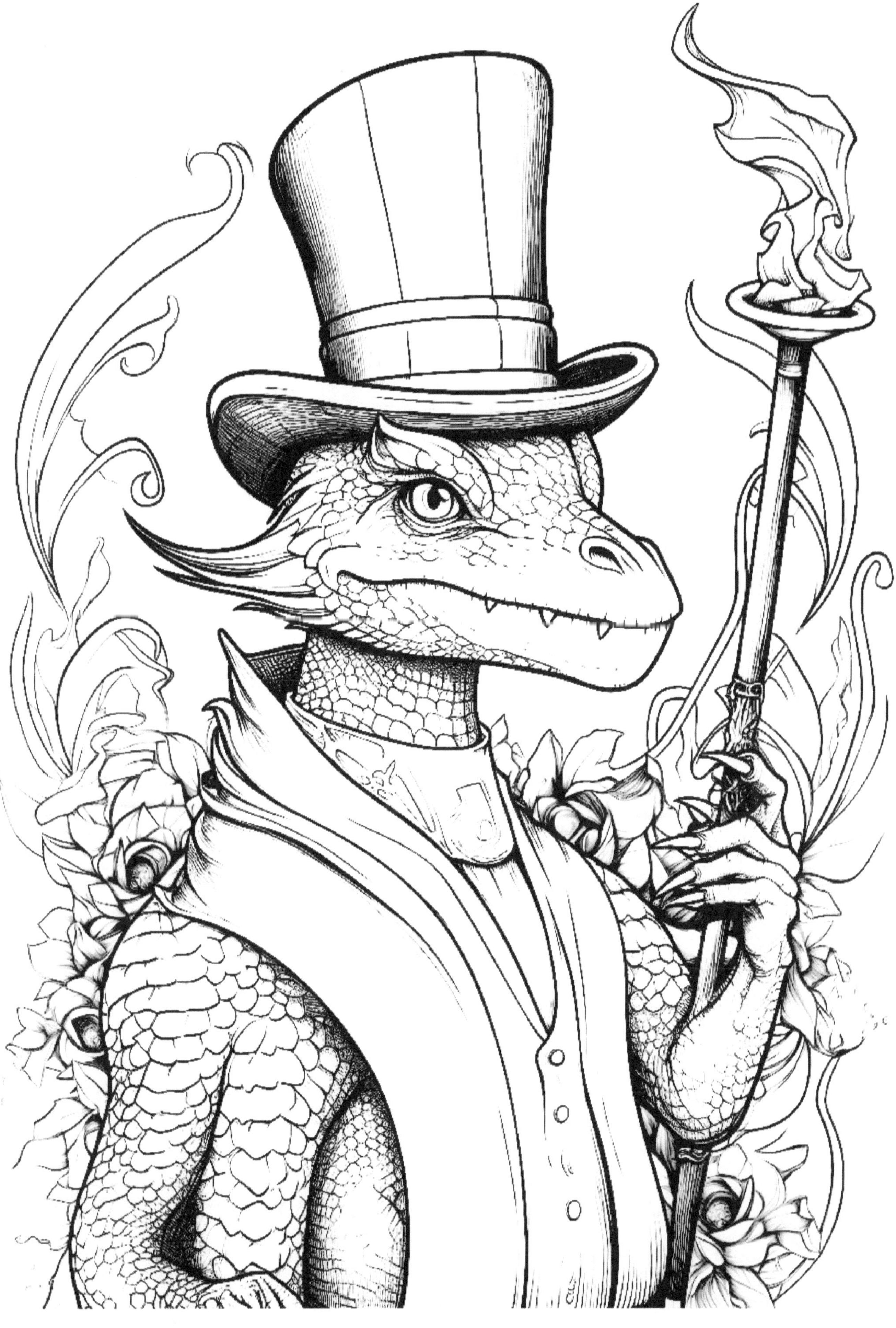

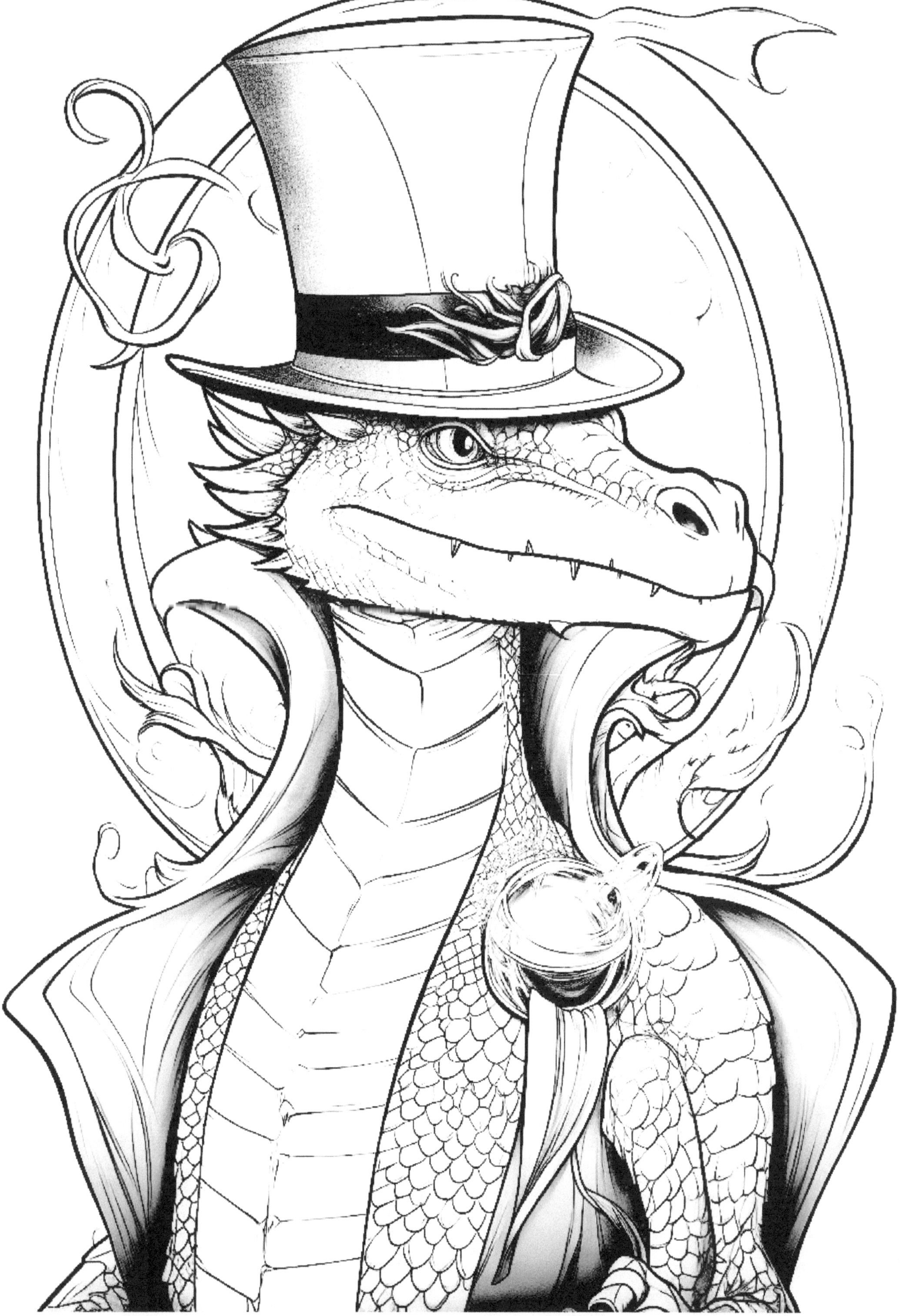

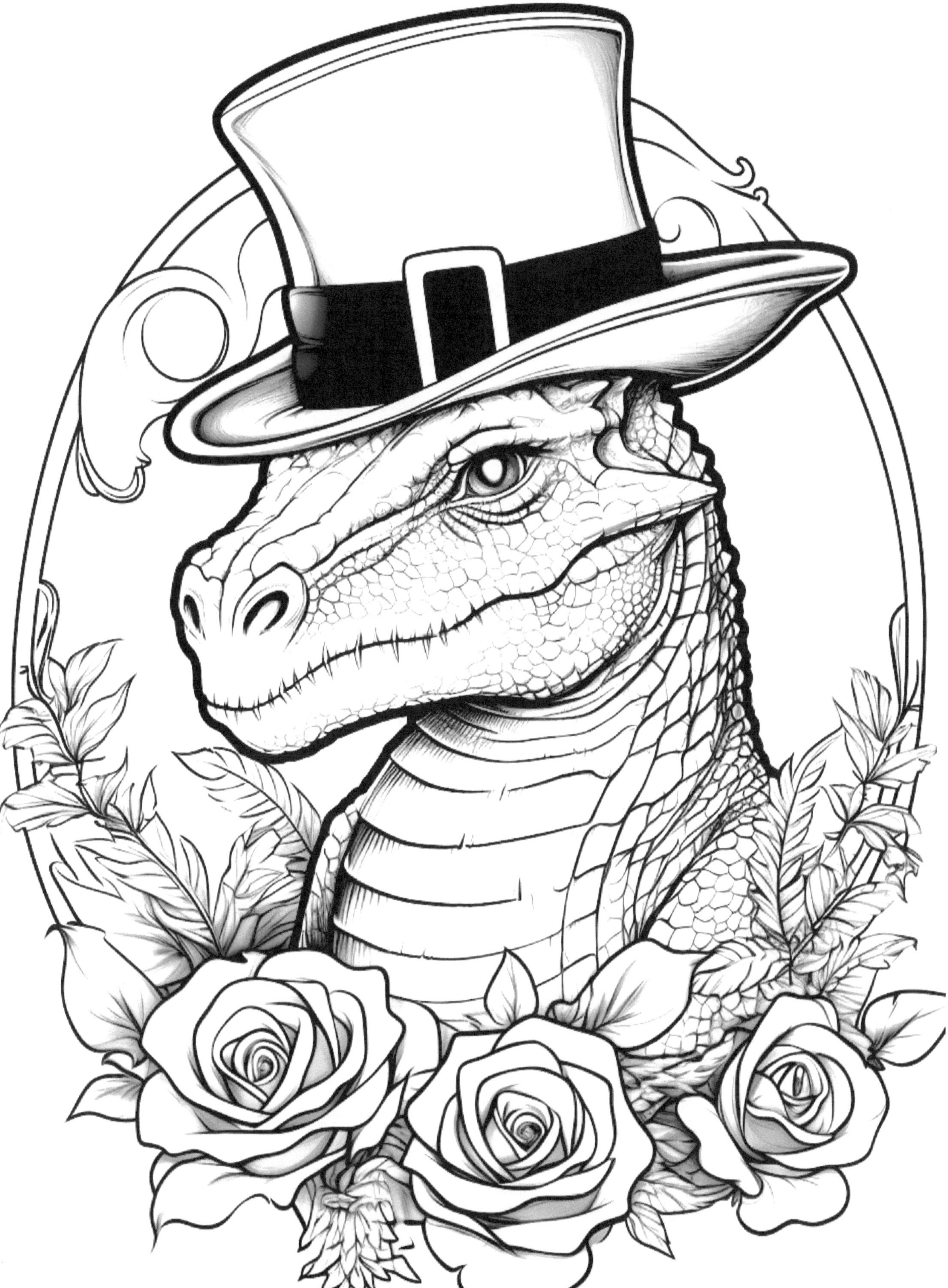

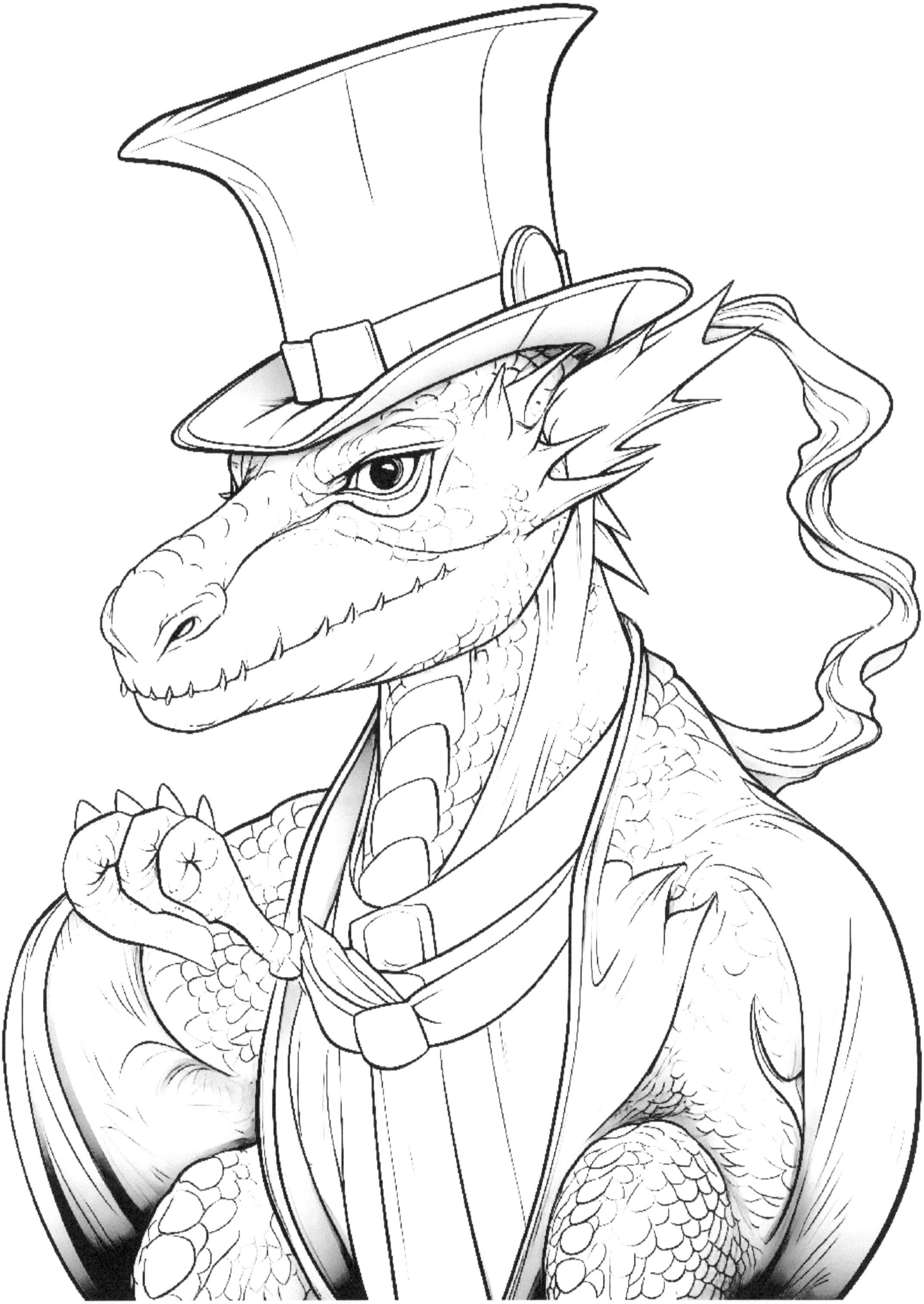

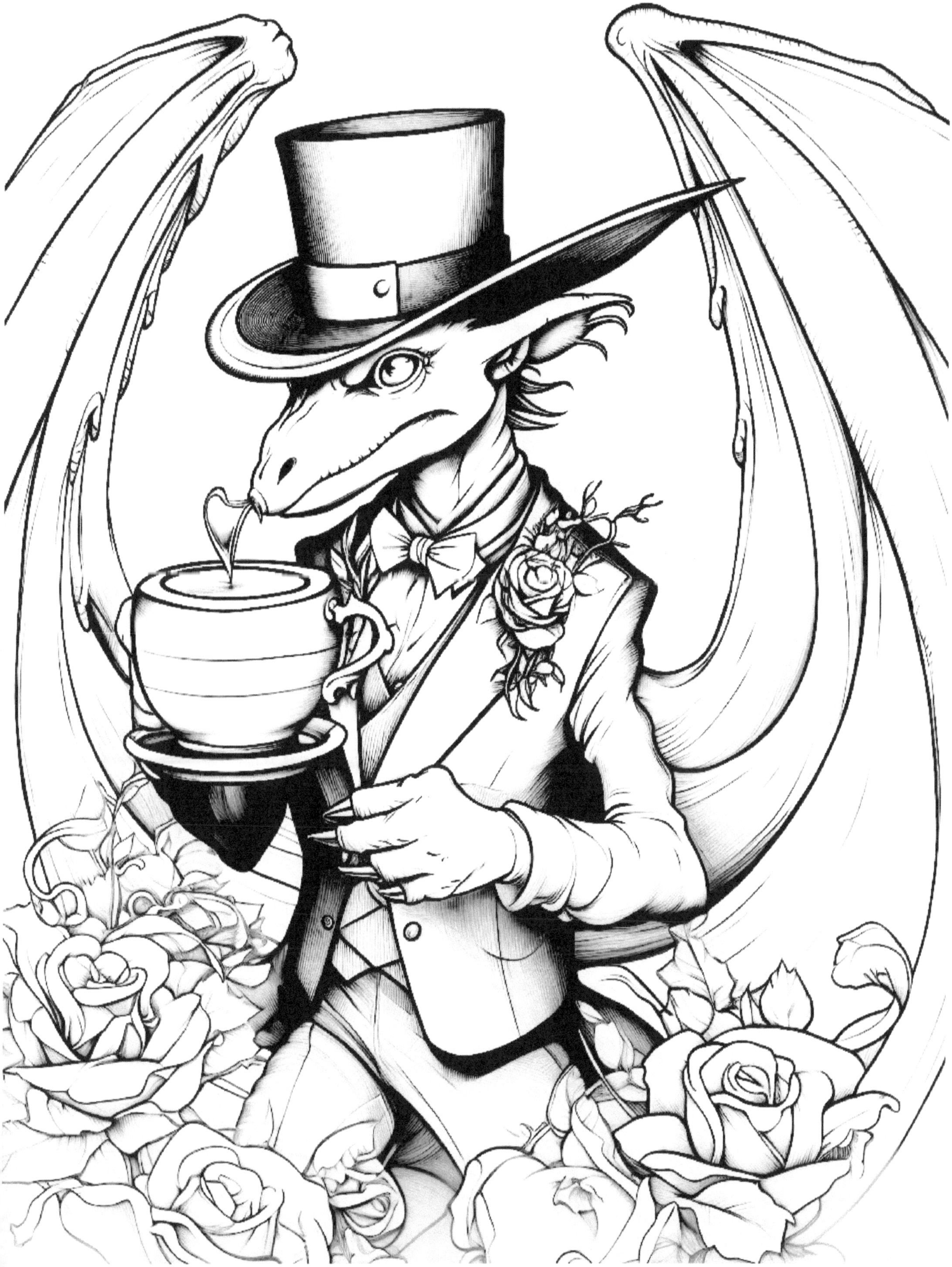

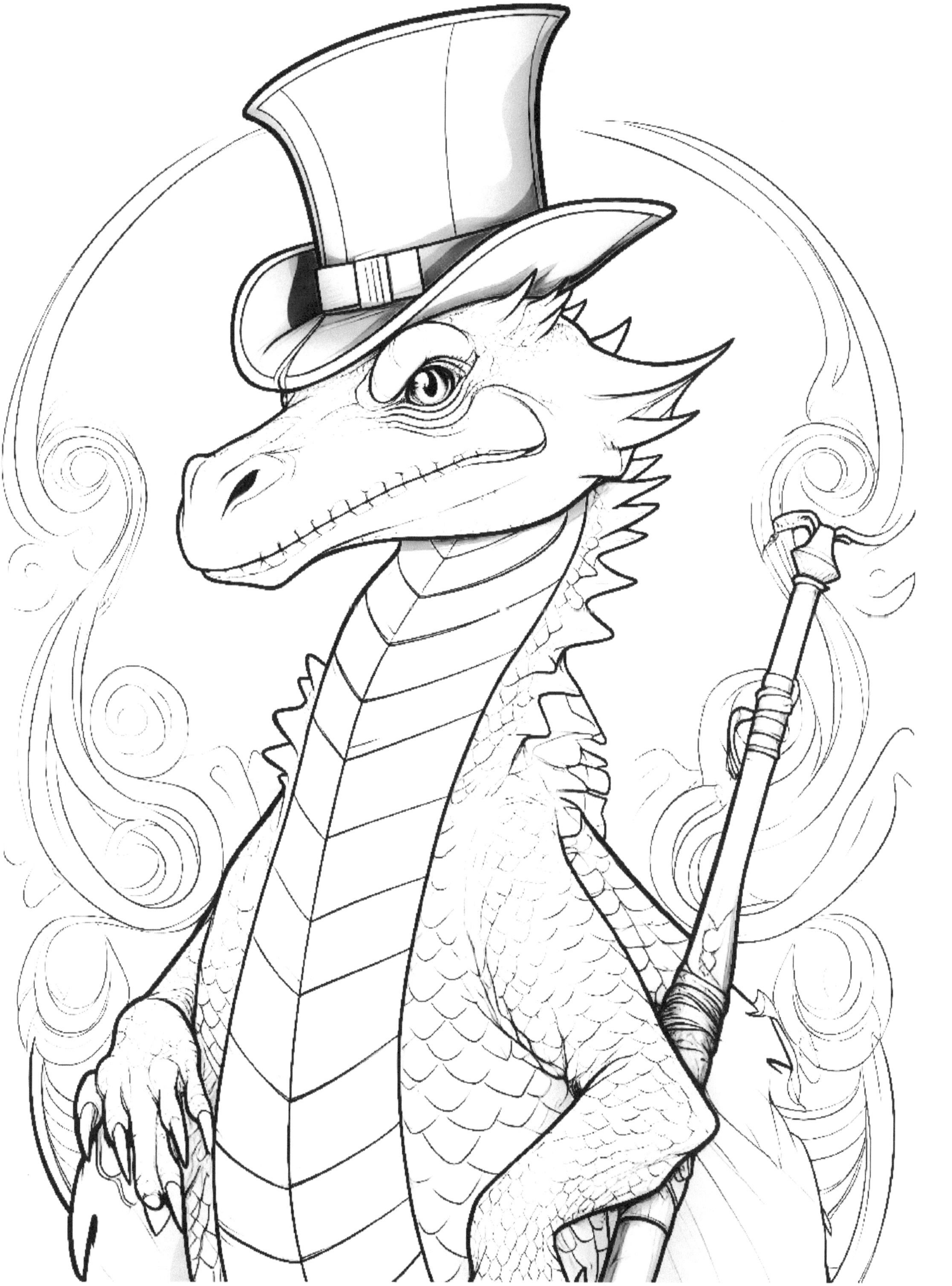

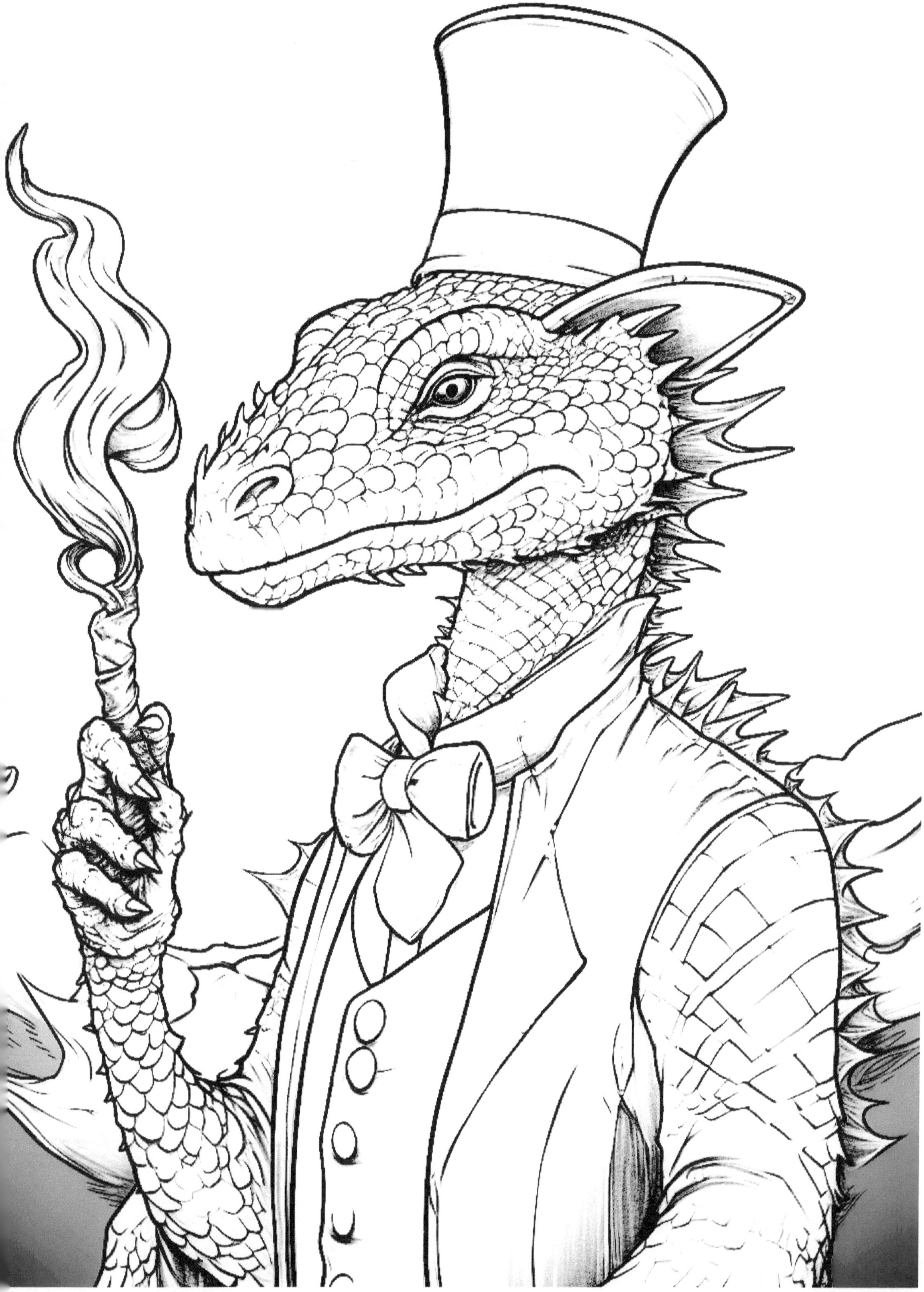

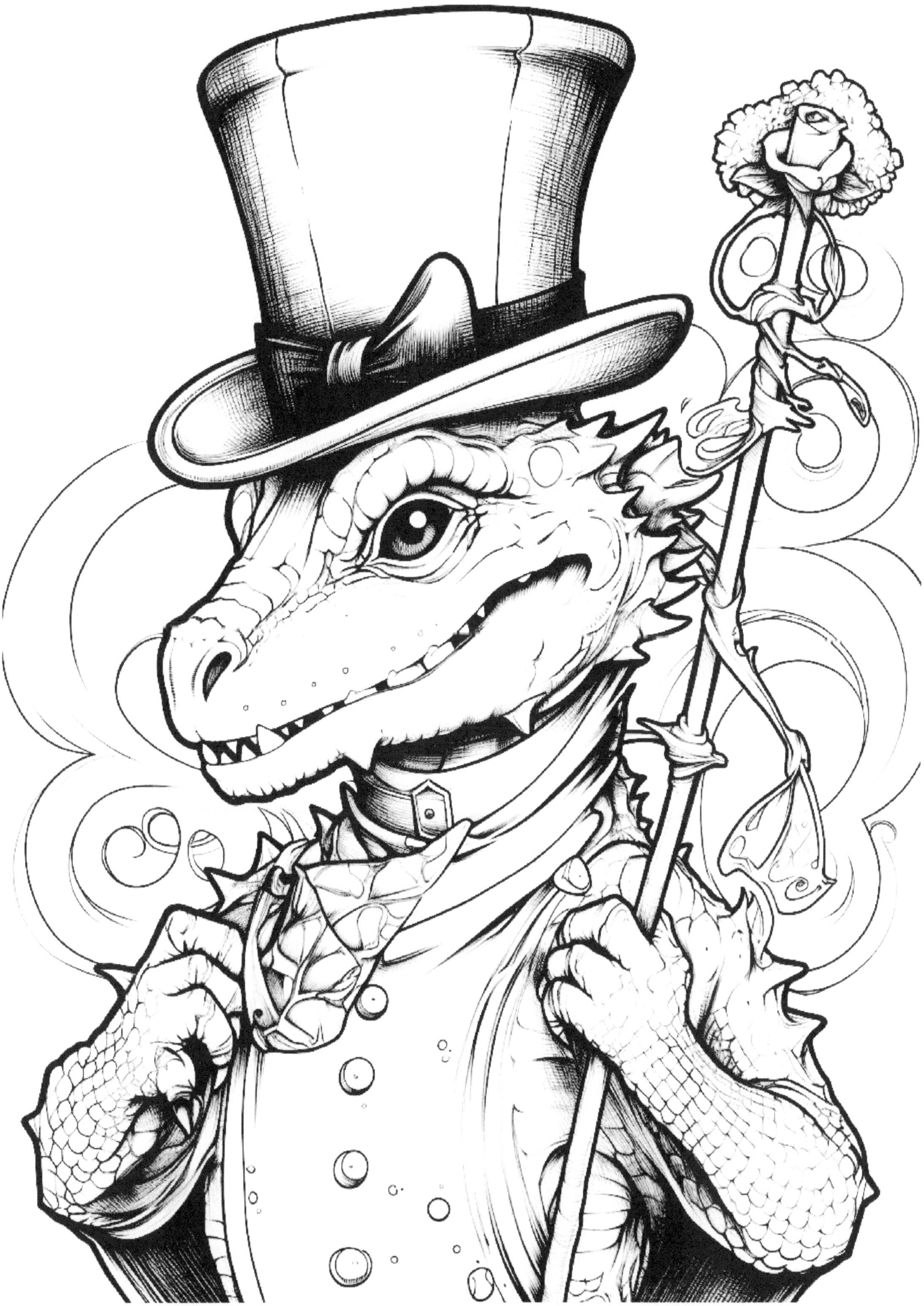

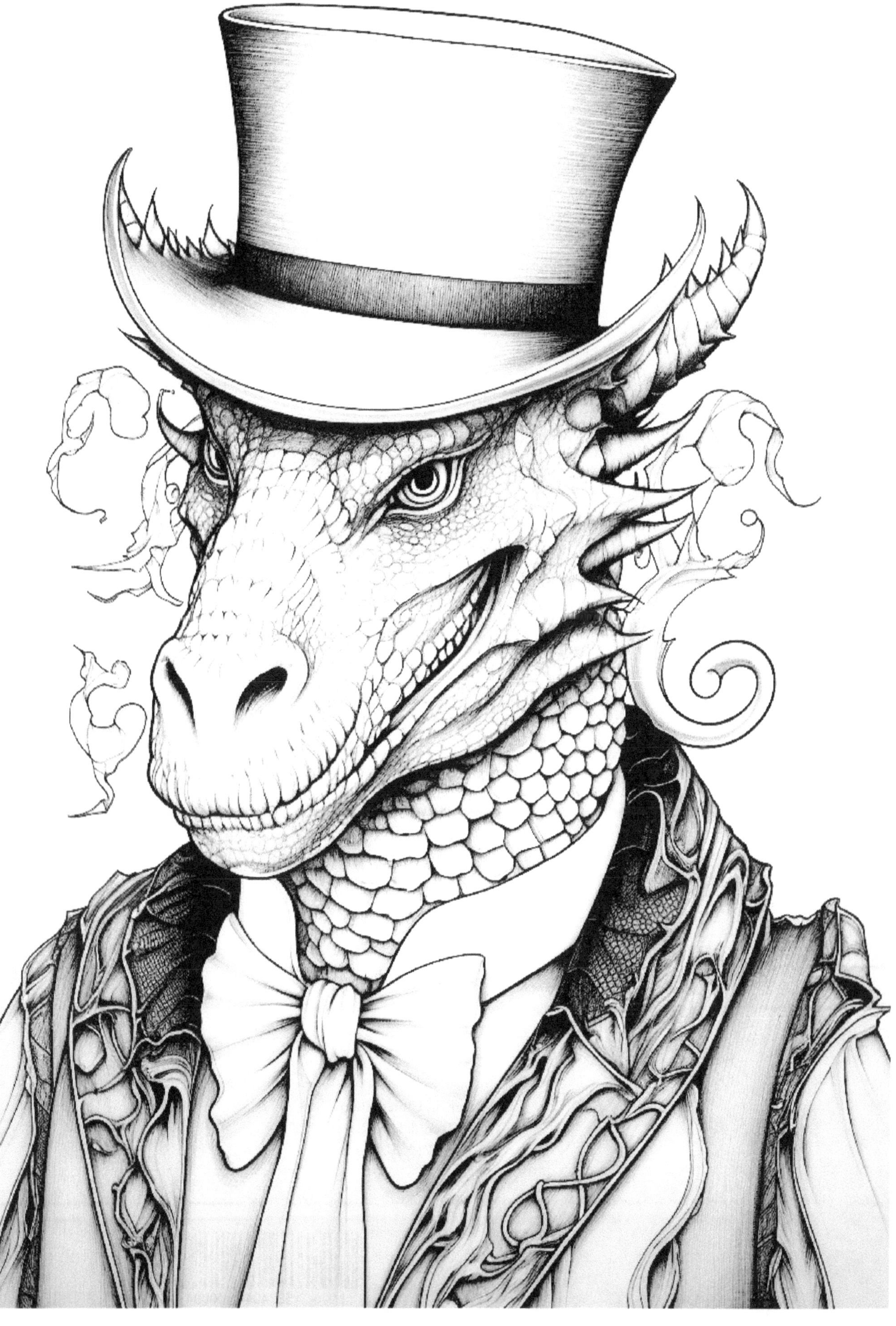

Made in United States
Troutdale, OR
12/14/2023

15874040R00084